Blue Walla

Sam McLeod

Library of Congress Control Number: 2006931094

ISBN: 0-9767664-2-6

Printed and bound in the USA

Cover art and illustrations © 2006 by Detour Farm Publishing LLC

Cover art and illustrations by Jeffrey Hill
Cover design and production by Integrity Design & Copyworks LLC
Book design by Tom Zebovitz, AlacrityAT
Edited by Candace Rose

This book is largely fictional. Any slights of people, places or organizations are unintentional.

To Walla Walla
Best,
     Sam

The Beginning

Hi. My name is Sam. Well, it's not really Sam..."Sam McLeod" is a pen name—not my real name. I took the pen name because I've always wanted one and have always liked the name "Sam."

Some folks think that you'd only use a pen name if you had something to hide. So, to put down unflattering speculation, I usually add that I don't have anything to hide—that the pen name is not part of a ploy to conceal anything.

Unfortunately, a few months ago I did a really embarrassing thing—nothing illegal or immoral, just really embarrassing. I'm not telling anybody about it. So, now I do have something to hide—just one measly little thing—and it's become another reason to keep the pen name.

Occasionally some niggling bookish type will take me aside. He'll tell me that a right-thinking author does not tell folks that he's using a pen name—that it's just "not done." He'll pontificate on the advantages of anonymity and then, in the very next breath, he'll tell me how Samuel L. Clemens used the pen name "Mark Twain" to hide his identity.

"Is that right?" I say.

Oh sure, I'd like to believe that my pen name will remain untarnished by the flaws of the underlying human being. I'm happy to take advantage of some temporary anonymity, but I don't count on it.

In today's publishing world there are literally hundreds of new books arriving on bookstore shelves each day. Something over 20 new books are published every hour. So, an author who sends a few copies of his new book off to some bookstores, and sits around waiting for the acclaim and recognition he so richly deserves, is doomed to live out the rest of his life in the midst of hundreds of his books piled up to the ceiling of his living room. He will never sell books to anybody but his mother.

No, an author has to get out there and do book signings, and radio shows, and speaking engagements, and TV shows and all manner of shameless promotion to get his book known so he can sell those books and save his nap sofa from becoming a permanent book repository.

I've even heard of one little-known author who made life-sized cardboard cutouts of himself and took them around to shops in his hometown so folks walking around would see him everywhere they went. A bit over the top, don't you think?

Now, if an author gets out there in front of the public and parades around using a pen name without owning up to it, at some point he'll run into somebody he knows, and that acquaintance will point at him and call out his given name and everybody standing around will gasp and cup their hands over their mouths like that's somehow an appropriate response, and the author's cover will be blown forever... And you know what's worse? He'll look like he has been hiding something.

So, to avoid that horrible fate, I just tell everybody that Sam McLeod is a pen name. I like the name. And now, I also use it on the off-chance that my anonymity holds for a while longer.

* * * * *

In my previous books I've brought you good and loyal readers up to date on what's happening in the McLeod family. What I've found is that telling folks all about my family is viewed by some as an invitation to catch me on the street and tell me all about their families. As you'd probably guess, these encounters are time-consuming and—how do I say this?—mostly boring.

This got me to thinking that maybe I should walk a mile in your shoes and see the McLeod family update from your point of view. When I did, it seemed pretty clear to me that you might not want me to fill this book to overflowing with McLeod family doings.

So, I went and asked some folks their druthers. Most said, "Oh no, no, no... we really like the McLeod family updates in your books." And then there was a long silence during which it became obvious, even to me, that they were hoping to change the subject.

Okay, I can take a hint. For those of you who are

interested, I have included "A Brief Update on the McLeod Family" on page 213 of this book. You can go there and read it or you don't have to; it's entirely up to you.

For those of you who are going to skip the update, let me just say that we're all doing fine. I have a slight cold—just sniffles and a scratchy throat—but it's not debilitating.

* * * * *

A few weeks ago I played storyteller at a local ladies' club. After the talk, one of the nice ladies in the audience came up to me, introduced herself and told me how much she had enjoyed the story—that she'd been entertained and was thankful for the amusement.

But then she asked whether there had been some little message in my talk—some little nugget of wisdom that she could take home with her and think on for a few days and come away from the whole experience a better person. She went on to say that if there had been such a nugget, she was afraid it had gone by her; she thought that maybe she'd been whispering to one of her tablemates and had missed it.

Well, I put her mind at rest. I said no, there hadn't been any such nugget. I said I considered myself fortunate to entertain, and that edification was a stretch—too much of a stretch for a simple-minded fellow like myself.

You should have seen the disappointment in her face.

So, I hope you are not expecting this book to be

both entertaining and enriching. I'm worried about whether you'll even find it entertaining.

* * * * *

Here's another thing I need to take care of before we get going: Several members of my family have button-holed me since my last book came out and they want me to devote this book to setting the record straight on some stuff. Well, I don't think you'd appreciate an entire book full of their views and corrections, but, if you don't mind, I'll go ahead and get this out of the way now—just a short summary of their perspectives on things.

Annie, my wife and best friend, wants you to know that she is not the snoop I make her out to be—suggesting to you that she's always looking over my shoulder to see what I'm writing. She says she is merely interested in what I am telling folks, and thinks readers will appreciate the candor and truth she brings to the party. She says that if you were here living at the farm with us, you'd get a much more balanced view of our relationship and the positive influence she is regularly having on me. She is pretty sure you'd thank her if you knew what my books would be like without her involvement.

Marshall, our youngest daughter and still a college student, says she is okay with the way I have portrayed her so far. She does, however, hope I'll leave her out of future books, including this one, because we should all "quit while we're ahead."

Jolie, our middle child, says that you should know

how sophisticated and worldly she has become since moving to New York. Otherwise, she agrees with her younger sister and thinks I should quit playing with fire.

Come to think of it, all of the ladies in my family think it is just a matter of time until I put something in one of my books that will really tick somebody off.

Summer, our eldest daughter, says she approves of my using words like "clever" and "independent" to describe her and is glad I've quit telling folks that she is mostly biding her time until her boyfriend proposes to her. She admits a serious interest in marriage but wants folks to understand that, even in a committed relationship, she intends to continue being "clever" and "independent" as well as "athletic" and "adventurous."

Okay... I believe that's a fair representation of the family's views.

Jolie's friend, Elisabeth, would like you to know that her name is spelled with an "s" instead of a "z." She apparently sulked for a while about the error in my last book, but seems to be doing fine now.

There is only one other person who regularly accosts me with her book-related disappointment. Mary is a friend of ours who agreed to pose as Naked Girl on the cover of the last book. If you haven't read *Bottled Walla* yet, you might want to go out and buy a copy and look at the picture on the front cover. There you will see Naked Girl (a character in the book). That's Mary.

Her complaint is that she has not gotten as many flattering comments as she had expected and thinks the picture of her on the cover must be too small for folks to make out clearly. There's not a lot I can do about that now unless you good and loyal readers buy a bunch of the *Bottled Walla* books. Then I'll have to do a second printing and may be able to adjust the cover art to give Mary a bit more prominence. That'd make her very happy.

* * * * *

And here's the last thing we need to deal with before we can move on with our lives: I have to tell you that I grew up in the South. I talk a little "slow"—partly because everybody "down there" talks a little slow and partly because my brain seems to take its own sweet time formulating things to say.

I think there is a better chance you'll enjoy the book if you read it "slow" while conjuring up in your mind the picture of a narrator who is doing his best to get the words out but is struggling with them just a bit— which is unfortunately the truth.

So, here goes... I hope you are not one of those people who believe everything they read...

Best,
SAM

Southern Man

I have always wanted to be an author. I am now 55 years old and have been writing books for the past two years. So, for 53 years I thought a great deal about writing but didn't pursue it. This has caused me recently to wonder why a person would think for so long about doing something he'd love to do, without acting on it.

It is a good question, don't you think?

To explore this fascinating question I'm afraid I must digress. It's a good thing my wife, Annie, isn't around. She hates it when I digress.

As I have told you, I grew up in the South. Annie did, too. She grew up in Richmond, Virginia and I grew up in Nashville, Tennessee. We are both products of "southern culture."

Oh, no. I was worried that this might happen. Annie is here standing beside me now—looking over my shoulder. She is grimacing at that last statement.

No self-respecting Richmonder appreciates having her fair city's southern culture lumped in with Nashville's southern culture as if they were somehow the same. According to Richmonders, Richmond's southern culture is the real thing, and is much more refined and genteel than Nashville's. From the perspective of a Richmonder, Nashville's version of southern culture is tainted with country music, smacks of honky tonk, and is therefore inferior. I can assure you that Nashvillians disagree.

Thankfully, these petty feuds between southern cities are not important to what I'm about to say, so I'm going to lump the various versions of southern culture together here and just talk about southern culture as a general concept.

To my way of thinking, southern culture is mostly defined by two things—southern food and the southerner's certain knowledge of "the right way to live." Every southerner arrives on this Earth knowing the right way to live.

Now, food is a very positive aspect of southern culture. Unfortunately, food is not the subject of this story. I'd love to spend some time talking about fried chicken and the "right way" to make deviled eggs (the kind my mother makes), and potato salad, and Jell-O salads made with Coca Cola, but without the nuts. (I have never understood why anyone would want to ruin a perfectly good Jell-O salad by adding nuts, or even worse, chopped celery. What are these ladies thinking?) And if we were talking about southern foods, which we're not, we'd talk about country ham and biscuits, shrimp and grits, strawberry pie, and pecan pie...

No, the part of southern culture I want to talk about here is every southerner's in-bred knowledge of the right way to live. We southerners *know* the right way to live. And when you know the right way to live, it is not just okay, it is incumbent upon you to go about doling out great gobs of unsolicited advice to other folks on how they should be living their lives. Knowing the right way to live is a great responsibility. As you will see, the words "must" and "should" figure very prominently in the southerner's vocabulary because there are a great many "musts" and "shoulds" in living your life the right way.

I will not try to speak for southern girls. I did not grow up as a southern girl. Maybe Annie would like to write on that some day.

I will only speak for the boys. And this is what I know for sure: From the time you are able to understand, most of the adults who take part in your upbringing will impress upon you the great importance of doing well in your studies, excelling at sports, and being the president of any organization that will have you, so you can put this important information in your college applications and get into "one of the better schools"—preferably a good southern one.

From your first day at a fine southern college, you must study the classics and, after four (or sometimes, five) years, take a liberal arts degree on your way to becoming a well-rounded person. At this point you will be prepared for graduate school in medicine, or law or business. That's it—three choices—doctor, lawyer or banker. You may pick any of the three, but if you are going to live your life the right way you will become one of the three.

Along the way, you must find a nice girl from a good family and you must court her respectfully. Then you must marry her, and the two of you must have three children.

Producing and bringing forth fewer than three children suggests a bit of marital primness and a cooler-than-truly-southern current in the blood. Genuine southern blood is quite warm.

Producing and bringing forth more than three children suggests excess heat in the blood and a certain lack of restraint. Genuine southerners know how to manage the heat in their blood.

Delivering three children into the world demonstrates to onlookers (and there are plenty of these around) an appropriate level of heat in the blood and just the right amount of restraint. It shows good balance in the marital estate.

Once you have your three children, you must go live in a big house in one of the better neighborhoods in town. After you settle into your big house, you must raise your children, encourage them to "live the right way," send them off into the world and wait patiently for your nine grandchildren.

As a reward for living your life the right way, you may then spoil your grandchildren for a while before you die.

Now, don't get me wrong. This stultifying, narrow-minded approach to life has its benefits. It produces a well-ordered society of mostly bankers and lawyers and doctors, almost all of whom marry nice girls from good families who bear promising southern children, and keep up those big houses, and prepare fried chicken, potato salad and Jell-O salad made with Coca Cola. Such a society has its good points.

But southern society does not encourage a career in

the arts—no starving artists, no dancers for heaven's sake, and no writers, unless of course you are the reincarnation of William Faulkner and achieve great acclaim that shines brightly all over the South and you promise to portray southerners as uniformly wonderful people. The culture is certainly rich enough to produce writers. It's just not encouraged.

So, we southerners leave careers in the arts to New Yorkers and West Coast people; in fact, we encourage these unfortunate non-southerners to take careers in the arts. How else will we southerners be entertained?

Miss Fleming

Now, in fairness, there have been a few folks along the way who've thought that there might just be a little more to life than is suggested by my summary. I would like to introduce you to my third grade teacher, Miss Fleming (because that's what she was way back when... a "Miss"... we did not yet know that there was a "Ms." alternative).

Miss Fleming taught third grade at HG Hills Elementary School just off Davidson Road in Nashville, Tennessee. She was a long, tall, strikingly beautiful woman with raven black hair and big green eyes that saw the world through glasses framed in red and shaped like the wings of a butterfly. She wore dangling earrings so laden with hearts and moons and giant yellow balls that I often wondered how her ears stayed on the sides of her head.

She also wore colorful blouses and flowered skirts and sometimes her sparkling red shoes, the ones she called her Wizard of Oz shoes. According to the assessment of parents overheard by us impressionable children, she was a bit of a free spirit—maybe a little too much of a free spirit. But we kids knew her as a fun lady who made school an interesting and lively place to be.

I had a massive crush on Miss Fleming... all of us boys did. I had to beat up my friend Brian on the playground one day because he kept on saying that Miss Fleming liked him better, even after I'd warned him not to say that ever again.

Occasionally, Miss Fleming would bring her flute to class and play for us. She played mostly happy songs but occasionally played a tune that'd bring you to the edge of tears on a load of sadness. Miss Fleming could do that a man; she could train that flute on a fellow's emotions and play them every which way to Sunday.

Now, before I go on about Miss Fleming, I need to take a little detour. It is a bad habit of mine. Don't tell Annie. She hates it when I take little detours.

The Gift

In the McLeod household way back there in Nashville, Tennessee where I grew up, we had our own way of doing Christmas. We had our holiday rituals just like everybody else.

I know I told you that producing three children is optimal but I am at the point where I must admit that my parents had five children—a fact that pushed our family to the fringes of southern society. It is a tough thing to reveal in front of all my good and loyal readers, but it is essential to the story.

My parents had good excuses for their indiscretions... or so they said. They wanted a girl and they kept getting boys. I am the oldest of five boys. After the third of us boys was born, my parents figured they'd give it one more go; and after the fourth of us boys was born, my parents decided they'd give it one more go; and after the fifth of us boys was born, they threw in the towel and said to hell with it, and got off the baby boy merry-go-round.

At Christmas, my grandparents on my father's side of the family, Mimi and Grandaddy, and my aunt, Wiese, would pile into the house with us for the Christmas festivities. It was right cozy. Some might say crowded.

The festivities went on for days, but the focus was on Christmas morning—the biggest day of the year for us boys.

We boys were sequestered in three bedrooms way off at one end of our rambler of a house while my parents and any guests were quartered way off at the other end of the house—as far from our rowdiness as they could get. Notwithstanding the considerable separation, my mother somehow anticipated our first stirrings on Christmas morning, which were a good bit earlier than was acceptable to the rest of the adults in the house.

She'd show up at our bedroom doors and herd us all into one room where we were instructed to wait patiently and quietly—something we could not do— while the adults got up, showered, dressed, and assembled around the Christmas tree in the living room with

their cups of coffee.

Once the adults had taken up their positions and settled in—a process that we boys judged mostly interminable—my mother would reappear at our holding room door and announce, "Okay, boys…"

She didn't have to finish the sentence, and as far as I know she never did. As soon as she cracked the door, we boys went tearing down a long hall, flying into the living room where—my, oh my—there were toys as far as the eye could see.

Santa never wrapped our presents and there were no names attached to the new toys. Somehow my mother knew which toy went with which boy. She'd stand in the middle of the living room and direct traffic, "Larry, that's your new tricycle over there… Gary, that's your toy fire engine over there... etc, etc." Somehow she knew what Santa had intended.

My father camped out behind the movie camera next to the huge lamp that illuminated the proceedings and blinded any of us who happened to look his way—recording the event for posterity.

We boys scurried around trying out every toy in sight while our grandparents and aunt looked on and sipped their coffees.

But this particular Christmas I'm telling you about—the Christmas of my third grade year—was a little different from those that had gone before, because under the Christmas tree, way in the back, leaning against the wall behind the tree below the picture window, there was one haphazardly wrapped gift. There was no bow and there was no card—just a scrap of paper scotch-taped to the upper left hand corner of the box that read, "For Sammy."

With some brotherly assistance, I gradually maneuvered the big box into the middle of the living room floor. I looked around to my mother for guidance.

She had a sort of quizzical look on her face and she kept cutting her eyes over at my father who had a big grin on his face and said, "Go ahead, Sammy. Open your gift."

After the wrapping paper settled onto the living room floor, I turned the box right side up so we could read the writing on the box cover. In print big enough for everybody in the room to read, it said "YOUNG SCIENTIST'S FIRST CHEMISTRY SET."

Oh, my...

Well, I am here to tell you that I was one excited little camper. Some of the older boys in our neighbor-hood had chemistry sets. I had watched them conducting their important experiments. I had admired the stuff that bubbled in the bottoms of their test tubes. And I'd begged my parents unmercifully for my own chemistry set—only to be told, "You're still a little too young, Son. You'll get a chemistry set some day when you're older."

And here it was. Finally, my very own chemistry set. I was a happy guy.

And then everybody in the room turned their atten-tion to the top right-hand corner of the box where, in smaller print, but still big enough for folks to see, the box read, "For ages nine and up."

Uh-oh... I was in the third grade. I was seven years old... not nine or up.

My mother's quizzical look turned into an exagger-ated frown. My grandmother and my aunt followed suit. The ladies in the room were frowning in unison. I looked back to my father who was looking at my mother and whose big smile had turned into a smaller, more judicious smile—really just the hint of a smile. My grandfather moved in to provide support with a cautious smile of his own...

There were two camps forming, and my elation flipped over into concern. It got very quiet all of a sud-den.

In situations like this my mother was the one who most often broke the ice. She said, "Sammy, why don't you boys play with your other toys for a while? Let's leave the chemistry set in the box for the time being. I think the adults need to move on to the kitchen where we will get breakfast going and where... I'D LIKE TO HAVE A WORD WITH YOUR FATHER."

Oh, how I hated those words. Whenever my mother used those words, it was generally not good news for us boys. My concern turned to anxiousness mixed in with foreboding.

Things did not look good.

After a while, my aunt called us boys in for breakfast. We all piled in around the circular mahogany table my grandfather had made in his shop. It featured a "lazy Susan" laden with country ham biscuits, cheese grits, scrambled eggs, red eye gravy for those who wanted to sop their biscuits in something, fruit, orange juice, a pitcher of milk, and coffee—an extra large Christmas breakfast just like previous ones.

We bowed our heads to get a better view of our plates piled high with food, and Grandaddy said grace over everything in sight and a whole bunch of things we couldn't see. And then, we dug in.

After some polite conversation about the quality and dimensions of our Christmas breakfast, my mother took the floor and this is what she said:

"Sammy, your father and I have had a discussion about the chemistry set. I don't really believe that you're old enough to have a chemistry set, but your father feels differently. So, I have reluctantly agreed that you can keep it. BUT... there are a few rules."

Rule 1: She said, "You may not conduct experiments in the presence of your younger brothers. When you blow yourself to Kingdom Come as I expect you will, I do not want you taking your brothers with you."

Rule 2: She said, "Sammy, you must conduct all of your experiments in the shower in our bathroom (meaning my parents' bathroom). The shower is tiled, floor to ceiling. There's a big drain in the floor. And there's decent lighting in there. You can keep your chemistry set in the bathroom linen closet. I will put in a supply of old rags to help with clean up. Do not, under any circumstances, use my nice bath towels for clean up or I will drown you in the toilet along with your chemicals."

And Rule 3: She said, "You may not wear your school clothes while working with chemicals—play clothes only."

Oh, my... it all turned out much better than I'd expected. It was a good day—a really good day.

Blue Gunk

Every day after school I raced in from the bus stop. I changed into my play clothes. I ran back to the other end of the house and into my parents' bathroom where I closed and locked the door behind me to keep my younger brothers out of harm's way. I pulled my chemistry set and a couple of old rags from the linen closet and set up on the floor of the walk-in shower. I fired up my Bunsen burner and conducted experiments until my mother called us for dinner.

Many of the early experiments ended badly. I had a lot to learn about following a chemistry recipe—selecting the right chemicals, measuring them out properly, combining them at the right times and in the right ways, and heating them just so over my Bunsen burner. There was a lot to know.

Unfortunately, I've always preferred to learn my lessons the hard way. I made a lot of mistakes. I produced a lot of ugly brown stuff and bad smells.

Occasionally my mother would come all the way from the kitchen, through the breakfast room, down the long hallway, through the den and to the bathroom door where she'd knock and say, "Sammy, are you okay in there?"

"Yes, ma'am," I'd reply.

"Well, Sammy, what is that bad smell? I can smell it all the way out in the kitchen."

"Yes, ma'am. I bet you can. That last experiment didn't go too well."

"Well, Sammy honey, would you take your pencil and mark in your chemistry book that your mother does not want you ever again to do that experiment in this house? The place smells like a sewer. I will not have my house smelling like a sewer."

And I'd say, "Yes, ma'am." And move on to the next experiment.

That's sort of the way things went for a long time—one mess after another. Until one day... one day when it all came together...

On that afternoon I measured out just the right amounts of chemicals, poured them into a test tube in just the right way, and heated them just so. The stuff in that test tube started to bubble—slowly at first—and then more vigorously—and then poof! A great white cloud billowed from the top of that test tube, gathered up under the ceiling of the shower and hovered there—a beautiful white cloud that just hung up there

21

like light fog.

For the first time ever, the smoke didn't smell bad… it actually smelled sort of sweet. The smell was not altogether unpleasant.

After the smoke cleared I looked into the bottom of the test tube where a glowing blue substance quivered for a while and then settled down into a hardened mass—a medium blue, iridescent residue. Oh, my… it was glorious stuff and it really did glow as if there were a tiny light bulb burning in the middle of it.

I searched my chemistry set for one of those small cork stoppers that fit in the top of a test tube to keep experiments properly contained. I couldn't find one, so I jumped up off the shower floor and grabbed a big wad of toilet paper, which I twisted and stuffed into the top of that test tube as I ran toward the kitchen where I'd find my mother. She was always in the kitchen—we boys knew where to find her.

Now, most of the time when we boys would run in to show our parents some great new creation, they'd say something like, "Nice job," and then go back to whatever they were doing. In fairness, it was a very reasonable response given that five kids can produce an awful lot of stuff that requires parental approval.

But on this particular day, there in our kitchen, my mother stopped what she was doing and knelt down next to me. She took the test tube in her hands and held it up to the light. And then she said, "Sammy… oh, my… this is beautiful. What is it?"

And I said I didn't know, but that I'd made it myself and it was the best chemistry experiment I'd conducted thus far.

And she agreed.

It was beautiful blue gunk... really beautiful blue gunk.

Show & Tell

I wrapped that test tube very carefully in more toilet paper and then wrapped scotch tape around the toilet paper so that my test tube—half full of beautiful blue gunk—would be well protected for the ride it would take the next day in my book bag. UPS would have been proud.

As luck would have it, the very next day was Show & Tell day in Miss Fleming's class there at HG Hills Elementary School just off Davidson Road in Nashville, Tennessee.

I did not normally have much to show or tell. But on that day I did. I was jumpy with excitement.

I sat in the row of left-handed desks that ran along the left side of the classroom as you faced the teacher's desk. Those were the days before political correctness. We left-handers were segregated off by ourselves.

I'd learned in first grade that if you sat in the last desk in the left-hand desk row, you were, as the crow flies, as far from the teacher as you could get. Generally this was the best place to be.

However, on rare occasions, being way back there in the corner of the classroom was a disadvantage. Show & Tell day was just such a day if you had something to show or tell.

When Miss Fleming announced that it was Show & Tell time, a sea of hands filled the air between Miss

Fleming and me. I had my left hand held as high as I could get it and waved it madly, but Miss Fleming did not look my way. She could be coy like that sometimes.

Sherry sat in the front row right in front of Miss Fleming's desk. Sherry was the teacher's pet and most always got called on first. So we all had to listen to whatever Sherry had to say. I don't remember what she talked about but I'm quite sure it wasn't very interesting.

Hands all over the room went up again. I waved my hand in the air with everything I had to put into it.

And then it was to Tom who was sweet on Sherry, sat next to her in the front row, and always got called on next. Once again, I don't remember what he had to show or tell—probably something he'd made with his Erector Set. Whatever it was, I'm quite sure it wasn't very interesting.

Hands all over the room went up again. If things continued the way they were going, I'd never get to show my beautiful blue gunk to the class and Miss Fleming—who would undoubtedly be so impressed with my inventiveness that she'd decide that I was worth waiting for and would not marry until I was grown up and of marriageable age.

But today was another good day for little Sammy McLeod because Miss Fleming looked right over that sea of hands to find mine and said, "My goodness, Sammy. You do not normally have anything to show or tell. Why don't you come on up and share whatever you have there in your book bag."

Holding what looked like (and in fact, was) a big

wad of toilet paper carefully in my hands, I bolted to the front of the room, stood next to Miss Fleming's desk, and faced my classmates. I started telling my story about Christmas, and my chemistry set, and working in the shower where I had my own private chemistry lab, and the bad smells, and what my mother had said about them. As I talked, I pulled toilet paper from the sides of my test tube, and about the time the last shred of toilet paper came away from the test tube and floated to the floor, I got to the part about finally getting an experiment right. I held the test tube up for everybody to see.

My classmates ooh'd and aah'd as they craned their necks to get a better look at the beautiful blue gunk that glowed from within.

Miss Fleming got up from her chair and moved to my side where she, like my mother had, knelt down next to me to get a better look. (She smelled pretty good.)

She invited the class to come up and gather around us and we peered into the test tube. We were all mesmerized. I'd lived with the beautiful blue gunk for about twenty-four hours and was still taken with it.

Miss Fleming asked, "What is it, Sammy?"

I said, "I don't know but it's beautiful and I made it all by myself."

There was a long silence.

Miss Fleming's eyelids started to blink a lot. Her eyes glistened with tears ready to brim up and spill over, and her lower lip curled up and quivered a bit. I thought I'd said something wrong, but Miss Fleming started to wave her hands and shook her head until she grabbed control of her emotions and squeaked that she was not upset, that it just looked that way, that she was actually as happy as she'd ever been. She just didn't look like it.

She said she had almost cried because she was happy. I don't think any of us kids had any experience with crying because we were happy. We'd have to take her word for it. It didn't seem right to me.

"This is a magical day," Miss Fleming said as she used a Kleenex to wipe up the black stuff that had run down her cheeks from her eyelashes. "Sammy, you have learned a very important thing about yourself. You must remember everything you can about making this beautiful blue gunk. It will be important to you some day... very important. It may turn out to be the most important thing you will ever learn."

I was confused. I'd learned an important lesson but I didn't really know what it was. I'd heard her voice and her words but the meaning had escaped me... or had it?

Miss Fleming helped me pick up the shreds of toilet paper and tape them back around my test tube.

And there it was... one lone but very clear voice suggesting that there might be more to life than "right way to live."

Living the Right Way

I went back to my seat carrying the beautiful blue gunk. I managed to graduate from the third grade later that year and, notwithstanding the great lesson Miss Fleming had taught me, went off to live my life the right way—the southern way.

I got the schooling and married the lovely Annie. We brought forth three wonderful daughters.

I've been both a banker and a lawyer. I managed to check off two out of the three acceptable career options on the great southern checklist of life.

We got the house on the hill with the lake views. We lived what many folks call a picture perfect life. By the time I turned fifty, we had done it. We had lived the right way.

And you know what? We were a little bored with it. There was a great deal of it that I had enjoyed, but I'd sort of done that. Annie said the same thing. It just wasn't for us anymore. We both felt like there was something missing... something that we still had to do... something burning to find its way out of us.

I sold my business. Our youngest daughter, Marshall, went off to college. And Annie and I decided we needed to get a new life—one where we could live the life we wanted to live, not the one others wanted us to live. We'd done that long enough. But that meant we had to figure out what we really wanted to do and be—and where to go to do and be it.

Now, my way of exploring these things is to get a bunch of books and find a nice cozy spot in a good coffee shop that also serves great pastries, and settle in to read. And that's what I did. I went off and read everything I could find on second careers, and getting in touch with your inner muse, and living in the moment, and paths to fulfillment. And I kept a journal of my thoughts—as if I could map it all out and come up with the perfect new life by thinking it through.

After several weeks of this, all of my reading and journal writing had not produced the answer—no road map for the rest of my life. I was little frustrated that the answer was not emerging from all of my self-study.

That's not to say that I didn't like the reading and journal writing—even if it wasn't answering my question. Oh, how I looked forward to that time every day. But the activity was not providing any direction... or was it?

And that's when the voice came back to me. The voice I had not heard for almost fifty years came to me as if by magic—Miss Fleming's voice telling me never to forget the joy of losing myself in chemistry experiments and making beautiful blue gunk. And, as I thought about the lesson she was trying to teach me that day, it all came clear.

It was the reading and the writing that I loved. It wasn't so much about the subject. Most any subject is interesting to me. It was the experience of reading and writing.

Writing was like my chemistry experiments done in a quiet place where I had my thoughts to myself without interruption. Most of my early experiments in writing produced nasty results and bad smells. Some of the writing produced beautiful blue gunk—something I could marvel at. But whatever the product, almost all of my writing time was satisfying. I found the work exhilarating.

So, there it was—a new direction in my life. After 53 years I'd finally figured out that there was more to life than living it the right way, and I was ready to do something about becoming an author. I would become a reader, an observer and a writer who'd sit in coffee shops that serve homemade pastries and compose creative works that would give me great pleasure and maybe even be of some interest to other folks.

And then the question was, "How do I do that?" I felt like I needed a plan. But that is another long story...

Food Stuff

Dear Good and Loyal Readers:

Because food is such a big part of southern culture, I have included several recipes in this book for your culinary enjoyment. If you try out the recipes and do not allow yourself to think too critically about the nutritional content of what you're eating, you will love the food—no fooling.

Occasionally I'll serve one of these dishes to a Walla Wallan who will say, "That wasn't too bad." And then, because I'm so taken with the compliment, I'll ask her if she wants the recipe. And she'll hesitate and then nod like she's a little unsure of something. And I'll give it to her.

A few days later a friend of hers will stop me on the street and say, "So-and-so says you gave her your thus-and-such recipe. Why haven't you given it to me? Do you like So-and-so better than me?"

So the recipes in this book are for anybody who's interested... and looking for opportunities to take more risks in her life.

Now, there's no suggestion in all of this that I'm any kind of chef or even a passable cook. These are just recipes for foods I like, prepared by people I care about. And when we serve these dishes out here on the prairie, it's clear that some of them are novelties.

I should also tell you that gathering up and testing the recipes was about as much fun as I've had in a long time.

First, I telephoned my mother who still lives in Nashville. We call her Coco. I asked her for a few of her recipes—her fried chicken, her pickled shrimp and her cranberry Jell-O salad (without nuts or celery). I told her I wanted to include them in this book.

Well, I waited several days, checked the mail regularly and kept coming up empty. So, I called again. She said she hadn't forgotten, that she had found those recipes, but was looking for an old recipe notebook she'd misplaced so she could also send me her meatloaf recipe, and her barbequed chicken recipe, and her roast beef hash recipe, and her... Well, I'm guessing that you've got the picture by now.

I had to explain to Coco that I just needed the three recipes I'd requested because they tied into stories in this book. I went on to explain that, while she does make a fabulous meatloaf and a scrumptious barbequed chicken and the best roast beef hash on the planet, I really couldn't use those recipes in this book because they didn't tie into any stories.

There was a long silence on the other end of the phone... You could tell that she was thinking... and then here it came:

"So, Sam honey, how hard could it be to add a story about my roast beef hash?"

Good question...

Then I called my aunt, Wiese, who lives in Jackson, Tennessee. I asked her for her strawberry pie recipe and her homemade mayonnaise recipe. She said, "Oh Lord, honey. I can write down the mayonnaise recipe 'cause I know it by heart. But the strawberry pie recipe could be a problem. Since I moved out of your Grandad's house to this old folks' home, things are sort of a mess and goodness knows what happened to my recipe file in the move."

"Well, Wiese," I said. "This is important. I need the recipe for my next book."

"Okay," she says. "Maybe cousin Anne will know what happened to that file. I'll check with her."

Last I heard, Wiese had checked with her cousin Anne, who thought that the recipe file might be in a pile out in her garage... but that Rosa Bell might have the recipe... It might be easier just to ask Rosa Bell... or maybe Sarah... What about Hattie? We all know Hattie has a great recipe for strawberry pie... And do you remember that wonderful strawberry jam she used to make?

Once again, I'm guessing you've got the picture.

I don't know exactly where it came from, but Wiese sent me the strawberry pie recipe and it shows up later in this book. It's a simple recipe and a real crowd pleaser.

And last but definitely not least, there's Jackie who lives way over in western Oregon near Portland. She and her husband, Arthur, are alpaca people and friends of ours through Annie's alpaca business. Jackie is originally from North Carolina and understands things like grits, turnip greens, country ham, and such.

She is also a remarkable cook. I called her up and asked whether she'd be willing to test several of the recipes and help me perfect them. And thankfully, she said she would.

Jackie told Annie and me a little story one day as we drove her to an alpaca show in Portland. She said that somebody had once asked Arthur and her what accounted for their long and happy marriage. Arthur and Jackie looked at one another.

Jackie piped up and said, "His wisdom."

Then Arthur piped up and said, "Her cooking."

Jackie has worked tirelessly on your behalf and has tactfully offered some nice improvements to the recipes that follow.

I hope you will enjoy them!

Country Ham, Biscuits & Red Eye Gravy

It is important to feed your soul occasionally to keep it in good shape. This is the perfect breakfast dish for that critical task.

This meal is full of fat and salt and therefore restorative in small doses... but, like so many things, potentially deadly if you overdose. It is a little like eating blowfish sashimi; there's a certain thrill to testing your luck.

We ate this dish only on holidays in the McLeod family household when I was growing up. My father was a doctor—a heart doctor—and didn't want us kids keeling over from blocked arteries on his watch.

Tennessee country ham is salt-cured, smoked and aged. It's delivered uncooked or cooked. You'll want uncooked, center cut ham slices for this dish—about 1/4 inch thick.

I generally buy my country ham from a small place called G&W Hamery in Murfreesboro, Tennessee. To get some of this unbelievably good ham, you'll have to call them up and ask for Bob. You can order over the phone and Bob will ship you the ham slices you'll need.

Another shop I like is Benton's Smoky Mountain Country Hams in Madisonville, Tennessee.

You can't go wrong at either place.

Annie is a baker. She doesn't cook much anymore. She says she's retired from cooking which means that if I want anything other than oatmeal for dinner, I'd better do the cooking. No, she doesn't cook much anymore, but she loves to bake. And biscuits are one of her specialties.

When Annie was growing up in Richmond, Virginia, Bebe was her second mother. On Monday nights, Bebe fixed fried chicken, mashed potatoes with gravy, a green salad with homemade blue cheese dressing, and her scrumptious biscuits. That's what Annie had for dinner every Monday night. Annie loves biscuits, learned the art from Bebe, and has written the recipe down for the first time so I could put it in this book.

Country Ham, Biscuits & Red Eye Gravy
Serves 4

For the Biscuits:
1¾ cups all-purpose flour
2 teaspoons baking powder
1 teaspoon salt
4 tablespoons cold butter
3/4 cup whole milk

Preheat the oven to 450°. Place parchment paper on a baking sheet.

In a medium bowl, mix the flour, baking powder and salt. Cut the butter into the flour mixture with a couple of knives until the dough is mealy. Add the milk and stir just until the dough forms a loose ball. Cover a smooth cutting board with a dusting of flour. Place the dough on the board, knead lightly, and roll the dough out to a 1/2-inch thickness. Using a 2½-inch biscuit cutter, cut out the biscuits.

Place biscuits on the parchment-covered baking sheet. Bake until light brown and fluffy—about 15 minutes.

For the Ham and Gravy:

2 tablespoons unsalted butter
2 slices of uncooked, center-cut country ham, about 1/4 inch thick
1/2 cup brewed black coffee

In a large, heavy skillet, melt the butter over medium heat and add the ham slices. Fry until nicely browned on one side—about 2 to 3 minutes. Flip the ham slices and fry another 2 to 3 minutes until the other side is nicely browned. Move the ham to a warm plate.

Add the coffee to the pan and deglaze. Bring the pan juices to a simmer, and allow to reduce to about ¼ cup. There's your red eye gravy.

Plating:

Slice the biscuits, placing two biscuit halves on each of four small plates. Cut the ham slices into biscuit-sized pieces. Place the ham on the biscuits. Spoon the red eye gravy over the ham until it runs all over the plate and starts soaking into the biscuits. Serve with a big cup of good coffee.

It doesn't get any better than this...

Welcome to Detour Farm

You may remember that I know a lot of Larrys. I know it's hard to believe, but here's a letter to another one.

Dear Larry:

Thank you for your letter. It can get a little lonely out here on the prairie. We're a long way from the neighbors. Letters from good friends like you help us stay connected. And yes, we are looking forward to your visit.

Farm life is agreeing with us. Occasionally a person who has read one of my books will stop me on the street in town and ask me how we are liking our new lives out here in the hinterlands and I'm quick to tell them that moving over here to Walla Walla is one of the best things we've ever done—even though we still mostly don't know what we're doing. We're very happy in our little farmhouse and are still taken with the view from our front porch. Aside from the towering cottonwood and ash trees hugging the river bank to our north, there's not much to block our view "up valley" to the foothills of the Blue Mountains.

We have several big, comfortable Adirondack chairs out on the porch. They all have seats wide enough to accommodate my wider-than-normal frame, and arms broad enough to accommodate a glass of red wine and a bowl of spaghetti and meatballs. They seem to encourage serious sitting and long-winded discussions about things that mostly don't matter.

Most nights—spring, summer and fall—Annie and I eat dinner out on the porch and watch brilliant sunlight fade from yellow to orange to pink to purple to dark. As the light fades, a cool wind kicks up south of us and slaloms down from the hilltops onto the valley floor where we live. It's our signal to haul out the sweaters and blankets and build a fire in the outdoor fireplace. The dogs take up their positions at our feet and BC, our newly arrived barn cat, stalks the field mice that hide in the woodpile out by the fence. Annie's alpacas pace the fence line trying to make eye contact with the Farm Boss until they figure out that she's not going get them a second supper. Pretty soon they go back to grazing or watching a coyote roam the riverbank; and all gets very quiet.

I enjoy porch sitting. I also happen to be very good at it.

Summer brought us a woven hammock from her teaching stint in Honduras last spring. It's hanging from the wood beams that hold our porch up. If I get tired of sitting on the porch participating in interminable chatter and let my mind wander toward taking a snooze in the hammock, I have found that it is best not to mention it. Leaving a group of chatterers mid-conversation to take a little nap tends to stop a conversation dead in its tracks. Folks go silent, look around at one another and shake their heads disapprovingly.

Instead of announcing my nap, I've learned to get up from my chair and pretend I'm headed to the bathroom. Fortunately, this kind of mid-conversation departure is culturally acceptable. Then I make a surreptitious detour through the house and out onto the other end of the porch where I find the hammock and settle in. If you appear to be sleeping when your deception is discovered, folks will be a little miffed but they won't wake you up over it.

Annie and I sat on the porch last night, built a fire, and watched a couple of big blue herons mousing around in the meadow out toward the far corner of the farm. We also watched a Great Horned Owl swooping in low over Yoda, our big-eared, low-slung Corgi, who was lying in the grass chewing on a stick just below the porch. That big owl was apparently interested in seeing whether Yoda might make a good meal. The only other detectable movement in the valley involved the wind chimes hanging from a nail on the corner of the porch, blowing this way and that in a breeze barely strong enough to generate a faint ringing—very peaceful. I'm sure we'll do some serious porch sitting while you're here.

Your guest cottage is waiting for you. And no, you don't need to bring anything.

We have had a goodly number of visitors since we moved out to the country, so we have a little experience now with what works. The main thing for you guys to keep in mind is that it's your trip and you're mostly on your own. Annie and I have farm chores to get done that'll probably keep us from touring around with you. (The animals seem to prefer being fed every day and do not take kindly to going hungry while we play with our visitors.)

We'll have dinner out here at the farm one night and probably go out for dinner another night. Otherwise, we'll help you get your bearings and point you toward all the fun.

Farm Rules

1. If you need something or can't find something or are otherwise confused about something, please

ask. We may not know how to help you, but we'll try. We want you to enjoy your stay.

2. Coffee, tea, juice, Annie's biscotti, fresh-baked bread and homemade elderberry jam are available every morning in the main house from 7am to 9am. We may or may not be here when you come in, so just help yourself.

3. There's a coffee maker in your cottage kitchen. Coffee, tea and snacks are in the cupboard. Water, juice, beer and a bottle of local white wine are in the refrigerator.

4. There are extra toiletries in the bathroom medicine cabinet just in case you forgot to bring something. We haven't yet found any of those really little bars of hotel soap, so I'm afraid you'll have to use a regular-size bar of soap. Just so you know, it is possible that some previous guest has used the soap by your bathroom sink. If you're a finicky type, just hold the bar of soap between your thumb and forefinger under hot running water for a while until you think all the germs have washed off. We are pretty sure that our guests are mostly clean, but in this day and age, you can never tell for sure.

5. There are great big nails in the cottage walls in some unusual places. Do not waste your time searching for the pictures you expect should be hanging there; they do not exist. No, the nails sticking out of the cottage walls demonstrate a rare nod toward frugality. Annie says we saved a bunch of money (and a trip to the store) by using big barn nails instead of buying coat hooks. Plus,

they add a rustic, sort of unfinished, feel to the place. (That is an understatement.) So, when you find one of those nails, feel free to hang something on it. That's what it's there for. You will surmise from the number of nails pounded into the walls that Annie figures most folks are traveling through life overburdened with a great deal of stuff that'll need to be hung up. You will also surmise that we had a huge number of nails left over from building the barn.

6. Please use anything else you find in your cottage. That's why it's there.

7. You are on your own for lunch. Folks who hang around the farm until lunchtime get put to work, so we've found that there are very few folks here at the noon hour.

8. Wine, beer and assorted other drinks are available every night at 6:00pm in the main house. If we're having dinner here at the farm, we'll usually eat at 7:00pm.

9. Dining Out—Some nights we go out to dinner. You're welcome to go with us or do your own thing. If you want to do your own thing, please do. No one will be offended.

10. If we go out to dinner, we just split the bill among the folks at the table. We started out taking folks to dinner or they'd take us to dinner, then the other couple would feel obligated to pay for the next dinner and... well, it just got tiresome. So, now we just split the bill and thereby avoid additional obligation and confusion in our lives.

Porch Sitting

1. The porch is always open.
2. First come, first served. If there's nobody sitting in the chair when you get there and you want it, it's yours.
3. Blankets are stacked in the box just inside the porch door. Grab one if you get a little chilly. Please put it back when you're done with it. If you leave it on the porch, one of the big white Pyrenees dogs—Sam or Annie—will shred it beyond identification.
4. And that reminds me of another thing: If you value it—whatever it is—don't leave it on the porch. It will become the newest dog toy.
5. If you'd like to build a fire in the outdoor fireplace, please do so unless the landscape appears parched. We do not want to burn down the farmhouse or the county. The neighbors would not be happy. So just exercise a bit of caution. We also ask that, if you build it, you stay up with it until it has died down to nothing. The winds out here can blow embers around in unpredictable ways.
6. And one last dog-related point: All of our dogs like to nose around in the human crotch. You are responsible for protecting your privates. You will find that a gentle command rarely results in disengagement. A forceful shove is about all that'll work, so just do it. You won't offend us or hurt the dog.
7. BC, our barn cat, will sit in your lap or on your shoulder if you'll let her. For whatever reason, she

is very happy perched on a shoulder and is adept at hanging on if you shift your position or even get up and walk around. She is happiest if you head to the hammock for a nap and let her sleep on your stomach. But, like the dogs, she can take a hint if you're firm in your resolve to keep her on the porch floor.

8. If you tire of porch chatter and head off to the hammock for a nap (after pretending that you were going to the bathroom) and Annie gives you any grief about it, just blame me. Then I'll be the one to get the sheet lecture from Annie and I'll nod my head like she is making a good point and then after a few days, life will in fact continue as if I'd never suggested such crass behavior.

Stuff To Do

1. Drink wine—There's a glossy brochure in your cottage listing most of the one hundred wineries within striking distance of the farm. Some folks tour wineries day in and day out while they're here and that is just fine by us, but there are plenty of other things to do if you wear out your palate.

2. Go for a walk or a bike ride—We've mapped out several routes for you. It's pretty flat for miles around the farm if you stay on the valley floor. We've got a couple of "beach bikes" for your riding pleasure. They have big baskets on them for carrying a picnic lunch or ferrying wine back from one of the nearby wineries.

If you are from Seattle or are otherwise fanatical about exercise, don't have a stroke worrying about whether you're going to be able to get in your regular fifteen miles of walking a day or whether you'll find enough challenge to get your heart pumped up into your personal training zone. There are some walks we can send you on that'll challenge you no matter how neurotic you are about physical activity.

3. Help out on the farm—This is definitely optional, but if you want to feed the alpacas, or clean out their stalls, or ride on the tractor, or take the ATV for a spin, or pull some of our infinite varieties of weeds, or fill up the holes that the dogs dig in the yard most nights, or haul the trash can a half mile down to the road, or move the sprinkler around, just ask...

4. Go shooting—We have shotguns, shells and a local gun club where we can go shooting if you're interested. If we're lucky, we may see some of our neighbors at the gun club, doing their cowboy shooting—an interesting sport where the participants dress up like Roy Rogers and Dale Evans and shoot real bullets at the kind of whirly targets that you'd expect to see in an arcade booth at the fair.

5. Go fly-fishing—Steelhead run in the Walla Walla River starting sometime after Thanksgiving. You'll need a fishing license (which you can get here in town or order over the Internet) but we have everything else you'll need right here at the farm. So you can leave your gear at home unless

you're overly attached to it. There is also great trout/steelhead/salmon fishing on other streams in the area. I know that The Fox has always wanted to go fishing with Annie, so maybe they can work out a trip one day while you're here.

6. Tour art galleries—There are a bunch of art galleries around the valley and five or six foundries where artists make huge bronze sculptures— many of them so big that the only place for them is a plaza in front of some very tall building. Lots of the valley's wineries also feature the work of local artists.

7. Go skiing—Try out Ski Bluewood just outside of Dayton, about an hour's drive from here. Stop for lunch at Patit Creek Restaurant or the Weinhard Café in Dayton on the way. Or have dinner at the WhoopemUp Hollow Café in Waitsburg on the way home.

8. Go to Pendleton for the day—About an hour's drive from the farm, this is the place folks around here think of when visitors say they want to see some real cowboys and work on their western wardrobes. On the way down, stop in Adams, Oregon and have breakfast at the Adams Store & Café. See the Pendleton Woolen Mills. Try on some cowboy hats at Hamleys. Eat the best sub sandwich in the universe at Como's Italian Eatery. Visit the Tamastlikt Cultural Center where you can learn all about the Indians in this neck of the woods. And take the Pendleton Underground Tour... highly recommended.

9. Go for a hike—We've got a great book you can

look through. The walking and hiking around here range from long strolls to rock climbing.

10. Go shopping on Main Street in downtown Walla Walla—Have breakfast at The Coffee Connection where Greg or Laurie will seat you. Enjoy a leisurely lunch under the awning at Merchants Delicatessen and tell Hippie Bob we sent you. Have your late afternoon glass of wine at The Bar at 26 Brix and maybe hang around for dinner if you're feeling the need for additional sustenance. Tell Mike and Krista we said hello.

11. Drive to Dayton and visit the Monteillet Fromagerie—They're the folks who make the goat and sheep milk cheeses. You'll probably have to have a glass of wine along with your cheese sampling while you watch the baby goats bound around out in the pasture. But hey, somebody's got to do it.

12. Go get a milkshake at the Ice-Burg Drive-In—The place can be crowded and there's a good reason for that. I always suggest that folks park and go to one of the walk-up windows to order instead of taking a chance on the drive-through where the person in the car in front of you is always ordering for an entire little league team. Not only does ordering for fifteen kids take a while but just as you think the guy's finally paid up and heading out (leaving the way clear for you to drive up and place your order), he decides he can't wait any longer, unwraps a burger, manages to dribble mustard and ketchup down the front of his shirt and has to call out for a box full of those flimsy

little napkins that individually are unable to do the job napkins were meant to do.

13. Go get a mid-afternoon snack—Look for the Taco Truck (La Monarca) parked on the corner of Rose Street and 11th Avenue. Try the quesadilla made with Walla Walla Sweet Onions. Or stop by the Worm Ranch and pick up a couple of tamales to go.

14. Visit the Walla Walla Farmers Market—It's open Thursday nights and Saturday mornings from May through October. If it's made or grown locally, you'll find it there. Get a cup of the best tabouleh between here and Marrakesh, and try the Walla Walla Sweet Onion Sausage on a bun.

15. Go into town after dinner—Listen to some live music at Vintage Cellars; take in a play at one of the college theaters; go to a symphony concert (the longest running symphony orchestra west of the Mississippi—yep, it's the truth); or grab a cup of coffee.

16. Sit on the porch and read a book… or just sit on the porch…

17. Take a nap.

*****

Well, I hope that helps you get a feel for what you're walking into when you come visit. We're looking forward to it. Tell The Fox we say "hi" and get her to call Annie if she wants to line up that fishing expedition.

Best,
SAM

Coco's Fried Chicken

It has taken me a surprisingly long time to learn how to make my mother's fried chicken. The recipe looks very simple, and it is, if you can master the frying. It's all in the wrist.

This is the fried chicken I grew up on. Virtually every major event in my life has involved fried chicken.

McLeod family gatherings were dysfunctional without fried chicken. One time, we went on a family picnic—a big family picnic with all the cousins, uncles, aunts, grandparents and a few unrelated interlopers—out at Percy Warner Park in Nashville—probably 30 or 40 people from toddlers on up to the nearly infirm.

The ladies hauled heavy baskets full of food out of the cars and put all that food out on several picnic tables—more food than double the number of gatherers could eat in one sitting. The men in the crowd carted huge coolers full of lemonade and iced tea to the tables and stood waiting for instruction as to where they should drop their loads. It was an impressive spread.

But wait! There was no fried chicken! Nobody had made fried chicken. You could hear the grumbling as folks circulated around those tables wondering where the fried chicken was hiding. How could they eat their deviled eggs and potato salad and Jell-O salad (without nuts or celery) and celery sticks loaded down with pimento cheese and ham biscuits and coleslaw and pecan pie and Wiese's strawberry pie... without fried chicken? It just wasn't right.

Grumbling turned to sulking in some folks; mothers

got a little testy with their children; a few of the aunts and uncles teetered on the brink of full-blown depression; and my granddaddy pulled my grandmother out of her lawn chair, folded the chair up, and announced that they were tired and had to "get on home."

The picnic was a disaster.

Thankfully, the mistake hasn't been repeated.

* * * * *

I have found that one of the secrets to making great fried chicken is to start with small pieces of chicken—a smaller bird is better than a big one. And in any event, breast pieces should be cut in half with kitchen shears. The reason for this seems obvious to me now, but it took me a while to puzzle it out. We're going to be cooking in hot peanut oil and the outside of the chicken must be browned to just the right color at a pace that fits with fully cooking the chicken. We are hoping for golden brown chicken that won't send diners to the hospital. Dark brown (bordering on burned) fried chicken is unacceptable. So, we need to start with smaller chicken pieces to maintain an appropriate balance between food beauty and doneness.

I brine my chicken pieces after I've cut up the carcass. I've tried all kinds of fancy brining liquids and have settled on the easiest one—salted tap water. You don't have to brine the chicken; but I think it makes a world of difference in the final product. So, if you are a person who possesses some modest organizational skill and can plan ahead just a bit, it's worth doing.

One last thing—I also think it makes a difference if you use peanut oil. It's a subtle thing, but meaningful.

Coco's Fried Chicken
Serves 4

Ingredients

8 chicken pieces with skin on (breast pieces cut in half)
1/3 cup plus 1 teaspoon salt
1 teaspoon freshly ground black pepper
1 teaspoon paprika
1 cup all-purpose flour
1 cup peanut oil

To Brine the Chicken

In a bowl large enough to hold the chicken pieces, put 1/3 cup salt and add about a cup of cold tap water. Stir until the salt dissolves. Add the chicken pieces. Then add enough cold tap water to cover the chicken. Cover the bowl and refrigerate for at least 2 hours. I sometimes brine overnight.

To Fry the Chicken

Heat the peanut oil to 350° in a large cast iron skillet.

Remove chicken from the brining liquid, rinse under cold water, and thoroughly pat the chicken pieces dry with paper towels. Put the remaining 1 teaspoon salt, black pepper, paprika and flour in a quart-sized heavy plastic bag, seal, and shake to mix. Put a couple of the chicken pieces in the bag, seal, and shake to coat the chicken completely with the flour mixture. Repeat with the rest of the chicken.

Carefully place the chicken pieces skin-side down in the hot oil and adjust the burner to maintain a vigorous (but not overly vigorous) frying pace. You want the oil to stay hot to avoid greasy chicken. But not so hot that you burn the chicken before it's fully cooked. It's a delicate balance. Fry the chicken 8 to 10 minutes on one side until golden brown. Turn the chicken and continue cooking another 8 to 10 minutes on the other side. Chicken is properly cooked when juices run clear after piercing the chicken to the bone with a fork.

Remove the chicken from the oil and place on paper towels to drain and cool. If you're going to season with additional salt and pepper, do it immediately after you take the chicken out of the oil. It'll hold the seasoning much better.

Serve hot... at room temperature... or cold... It's all good.

Living With Girls

Before I dive in here too deep, I have to remind you that I grew up with four younger brothers—no sisters. Before Annie and I got married, the only thing I knew for sure about girls was that you called one up, asked her to go out on a date, and showed up at her house at the appointed hour. Her father would meet you at the door, stare at you like you were some budding young rapist, and say that his daughter wasn't ready yet, but would be shortly.

That left you a few minutes with the dad—the obligatory few minutes that a girl would require you to wait just to be sure you knew that she was not too anxious to go out with you—that she was doing you a big favor... She'd be ready when she was damned well ready... and you should just cool your jets.

During your few minutes of terror with the dad, he'd tell you that his daughter was the light of his life, that he wouldn't want anything—and he meant *anything*—to happen to her... not anything that you and he might regret... and he'd look really serious about that. One time, while a dad was making that little speech to me, he pulled a baseball bat from the umbrella stand by the front door and twirled it in his giant hands... Message received, loud and clear...

And then your date would appear from down the hallway looking really nice with a big smile on her face, which was a nice balance to the big scowl that her father had on his face.

That's all I knew about girls.

And then I got married... Annie and I had three daughters ... and all hell broke loose. I've learned a lot from our daughters, but we don't have the space in this book to talk about everything I've learned. I'm sure you're very thankful for that. So, I've narrowed it down to just 5 things—just a few of most important things I've learned from my daughters. Here goes.

* * * * *

Number 1: *Never use the phrase "hookup" if you don't know what it means.*

When I was a kid, a "car pool" was called a "hookup." Every morning I waited for the "hookup" to arrive at our house and take me to school and then I ran out of school in the afternoon to find my "hookup." As our girls grew up and heard me talking about my "hookup" they'd cover their eyes, and shake their heads, and turn bright crimson.

One day Jolie took me aside and told me that I was embarrassing her and whatever "hookup" meant back in the olden days, it had some different meaning today and that I should stop telling folks about my "hookup." Okay, so I've stopped telling my "hookup" stories but I still don't know why.

* * * * *

Number 2: *Slamming a door is a form of female punctuation. It is a female exclamation point!*

Here's an altercation between Summer and Marshall that I overheard when Summer was 15 years old and Marshall was just 10 years old:

"Marshall, you slimy worm, if you ever—and I mean *ever*—take my brush again without asking, I will rip your heart out and stomp on it until your blood runs out all over the floor."

(I have found that girls can sometimes get a little upset with one another.)

Then I heard *clomp, clomp, clomp... wham!*

There's the exclamation point!... a door slam that rocked our house.

And then it was Marshall's turn: "Summer, you amorphous clod of dirt, take your stupid brush... I don't need it... Plus, it's covered in Summer cooties...

Then I heard *clomp, clomp, clomp... wham!*

Another exclamation point!

* * * * *

Number 3: *Parties are important... very important...*

I honestly had no idea. I don't care much about parties. I didn't when I was a kid and still don't. I'll go, but not because I want to. Once I get to a party, I can be pleasant enough; it's getting up the energy to go that stumps me.

When I was in high school, my girlfriend called me on the phone—a very rare occasion back in the olden days. Girls did not call boys. That's another thing I

just remembered about girls.

But on this one occasion she called me and invited me to her school's prom and because I was so surprised that she'd called, I said sure I'd go, before I thought to ask a few questions.

Then I learned that the prom was a formal affair, and I'd have to wear a tux, and I'd have to go rent one, and I'd have to get a corsage. I knew none of this. I had no one to teach me these things. And then on the day of the prom, I decided I really didn't want to go... and I feigned sickness... I actually did have a cold—sort of—so I called my girlfriend on the day of the prom and said I was sick and couldn't go.

When our girls started high school, Summer, our oldest daughter, was invited to her school prom. That started a cascade of events that she loved and her mother loved and her sisters loved.

Weeks ahead of the big event, we started to worry about getting a dress. There ensued endless shopping and discussion about this or that dress at this or that store and how much it cost and whether it was sexy enough but not too sexy and whether it had straps or not.

Then it was about getting the hair done and the nails... and what about the shoes? We never seemed to be able to find the right shoes. And then we found the shoes and oh, how nicely they went with the dress.

Then it was about inviting all of your friends over to your house several hours before the event and helping each other get ready while the moms and the sisters looked on. Every one in attendance was required to talk non-stop. I decided to go outside and power up the lawn mower to cut the grass; it'd be more peaceful.

And then the guys in their tuxedos showed up with corsages and everybody ooh'd and aah'd about the flowers—particularly the moms—and pictures were taken—lots of pictures. Then the girls left with their escorts to attend the actual party, which seemed a bit anti-climactic.

Summer enjoyed the entire process so much... Annie, Jolie and Marshall did, too.

And then I felt like a heel... I still feel guilty about calling up my girlfriend and canceling our prom date. I feel like I should call up now almost 40 years later and apologize... again. But maybe it's better to let that sleeping dog lie.

* * * * *

Number 4: *It's all about the hair...*

Annie, the girls, and I never had dinner together as a family without spending some quality time talking about hair. I always sat at one end of our breakfast room table in front of a big picture window. To our girls, that window was a giant mirror. Right in the middle of a conversation, one of the girls would remember that she had not checked to see how her hair was doing—for maybe the past 30 seconds—and she'd look my way—not *at* me, her very own loving dad—but beyond me to her reflection in that big window, to admire her hair.

And no matter what the topic, it could be turned to hair as in, "That is very interesting what you just said about global warming, Dad. We discuss global warming in school all the time. It makes me wonder what effect the extra heat will have on my beautiful, naturally curly hair."

And hair products... I still don't know how our girls manage to get into the shower without stumbling over the multitude of hair products.

When I was a kid, my mother introduced us boys to Ivory Soap. She'd put three of us in the tub and scrub us head to toe with a stiff brush and lots of Ivory Soap. It wasn't until I got married that Annie introduced me to shampoo—which seemed to work just as well as Ivory Soap.

And then we had three daughters and I heard about natural and active conditioners and aloe and jojoba and glow lotions and gels and five-step programs to healthier hair. I have, on occasion, tried one or more of these products when one of our girls would decide that she couldn't shower properly in her bathroom and needed to use ours, and would leave one of the six or seven critical hair products behind where I could get my hands on it. Near as I can tell, these products achieve about the same result as Ivory Soap... which means that, once again, I "just don't get it."

* * * * *

Number 5: *And here's the big one...Girls like to talk...Yep, it's true ...*

When I was growing up back in Nashville with my four brothers, my poor mother begged us to talk to her at the dinner table. She struggled to ask questions that couldn't be answered with a "yes, ma'am" or "no, ma'am."

Mealtime at our house was a time for taking on fuel. In our boy's view of the world, communication got in the way of that very important activity.

Then, Annie and I had three daughters, and we had to deal with a very different approach to the world. We had to develop special games to reduce the decibel level in our house, in our cars—in our lives.

We quickly developed and then played the "quiet game"—a lot. The challenge in the game was to keep your mouth shut. The first to speak "lost" and the last to speak "won." In theory, it was a very simple game.

In practice, every time Annie or I suggested we play the quiet game, endless discussion about the rules would follow—whether the game's basic rules should be modified or whether we should, at least, add some very important exceptions to the general rules—some wiggle room that would provide a basis for disputing a parent-declared loss.

We also had to review a bit of history before each game could begin—whether Jolie had cheated the last time we played and how Summer was always tickling her sisters to make them laugh out loud thereby causing them to lose, and how that should be prohibited because it wasn't fair, and on and on.

As the youngest and therefore least able to debate the rules, Marshall found that sucking her thumb and twirling her hair with her free hand helped her keep her mouth shut and was almost as enjoyable as talking—and she often won the game. It was a good lesson to learn.

The only time the quiet game really worked was when we attached a severe penalty to losing. Once we took a family trip to Disney World. We drove all the way from Richmond, Virginia to Disney World. It is a very long drive.

Annie and I gave each of the girls $20 to spend on the trip. (Now, before you start thinking that we were cheapskates, you must consider that we took this trip a long time ago—back when a dollar was still a dollar.) We told the girls we'd pay room, board and entertainment on the trip, but "things" would have to come out of their money and it was up to them to manage their newfound wealth. They could do with it what they wished—they could spend it or not as they saw fit. But, we also told them that it was a long drive and that Dad's sanity would be sorely tested so we'd probably play the quiet game from time to time *and the loser would forfeit a dollar each time she lost.*

I don't think they believed us until Annie made Summer fork over a dollar after her loss of the first quiet game we played on that trip. It was the most pleasant car trip we ever took.

At the dinner table we did not play the quiet game, but we did institute some decibel-reducing rules. For a few years, I sat in front of that big picture window and listened while everybody else at the table talked at once. Nobody seemed to be listening. I couldn't figure out what was going on. Annie finally said she thought we all needed to learn some manners. We needed to learn to listen while another human was talking... and not interrupt. I nodded my head vigorously.

So, the rule was that a speaker would have to raise her hand and be acknowledged by a parent before speaking... and that when a speaker took a breath, it was not an opportunity to interrupt. Thereafter, we mostly sat around the table listening to one person talking while everybody else's hands were in the air waving madly, seeking a turn to speak.

It was unbelievable, really. You could watch the pressure build up in those little girls while they waved wildly for air-time and then, when one was called upon to speak, the words would come spewing forth in a great torrent of important information.

* * * * *

So those are a few of the valuable things I've learned from living with girls... and I wouldn't trade a minute of my education for anything.

Sam's Shrimp & Grits

Done the "right way," this dish is not for the Pepto-Bismol crowd. After I celebrated my 50th birthday, my stomach installed a very sensitive smoke alarm. So, I've had to tone this recipe down a bit. Feel free to add more heat to the shrimp spices (say, 1/4 teaspoon red pepper flakes) if you can handle it.

Since Annie and I now eat more of our meals out on the porch, I am partial to meals that fit in one bowl. This dish is, to my way of thinking, the quintessential one-bowl dinner.

If you are serving this dish to a finicky eater, you will likely get a few questions about what's in the bowl before he or she will tempt fate with a fork. I have been surprised at the number of folks who say they don't like turnip greens and then admit they've never had them. Rather than fight an uphill battle with these skeptics, you might want to tell your guests that the greens are "southern chard." It's just a little white lie. Chard is apparently a fashionable leafy green vegetable these days.

You may also want to avoid the word "grits." There are plenty of folks in the world who hate grits but love polenta—even though they are the same thing. So, after you tell your timid diners about the southern chard, you may want to add that the shrimp lie on a bed of "creamy polenta."

This is the honest truth: One night several years ago, I had dinner with a couple of New York investment bankers in a trendy little Italian restaurant in downtown San Francisco. They were amused, in a patronizing sort of way, by my southern accent. Thankfully, I am happy to provide amusement for others if they will do the same for me, and these two were happy to reciprocate.

One of them said that his best friend was from the South, that he himself had gone to the South once, that the Ku Klux Klan had not molested him, and that he'd had country ham, biscuits and grits for breakfast while he was "down there." He said he'd loved the country ham and the biscuits but hated the grits.

I said, "Oh, really…"

And then his friend said he'd also had grits once and while he didn't hate them, he wouldn't go out of his way to get them again.

I said, "Oh, really…"

And then the waiter showed up with menus.

As we perused the day's specials, I noticed "Creamy Polenta with Truffle Shavings" listed as an appetizer for $12.00. "Wow," I thought, "$12.00… for grits… that's amazing."

I got ready to say something but before I could wind up my amusing southern drawl, the first guy said he was definitely having the "Creamy Polenta," that he loved polenta. The second guy allowed as how he'd probably order the polenta as well. I held my tongue and we went on to other equally scintillating topics.

Well, I'm here to tell you that two tiny little bowls of "creamy polenta" arrived and there appeared to be a dusting of powdered something on top. I didn't see any truffle shavings. There was a little sprig of parsley on the edge of each bowl and the bowls were set on huge dinner platters as a sort of frame for the dish.

They ate their "creamy polenta" with obvious delight.

As they ate, I ran the simple calculator in my head: 5¢ for the grits, 25¢ for the cheese, no charge for the parsley, and, let's be generous, $1.00 for the truffle dusting... Total $1.30. So these guys were paying $12.00 – $1.30 = $10.70 for clever marketing, a fancy Italian word and an admittedly nice presentation.

I was amused.

Now, it is possible that you will have to deal with a finicky eater from New York—the worst of all picky-eater worlds to fall into. So, maybe it'd be better if we just called this dish "Sam's Shrimp, Southern Chard and Creamy Polenta." I'll have to think on that awhile. I might also have to change "Sam" to "Samuel" if I go this way... and maybe "shrimp" would be better as "prawns." How does this sound: "Samuel's Prawns, Southern Chard and Creamy Polenta?"

I think it sounds a little snooty. Over the last 55 years I have scratched the finicky eaters from my lists of dinner guests, so I'm just going to say "Shrimp & Grits" because I'm inclined to stick with what's comfortable. But if you decide to dress up the name, I'm okay with it.

Sam's Shrimp & Grits
Serves 4

For the Turnip Greens:
1 pound de-stemmed, chopped turnip greens
1 large turnip cut into ¼-inch cubes
1/4 teaspoon red pepper flakes
2 tablespoons cider vinegar

1 smoked ham hock
2 cups water
1 teaspoon salt
1/2 teaspoon freshly ground black pepper

This is easy: Put all of the ingredients in a big pot, cover and simmer over medium-low heat for at least an hour. Even longer is better.

Remove the ham hock and allow it to cool while the greens continue to simmer uncovered. When you can handle the ham hock without burning your fingers, cut the meat from the bone and chop the meat into bite-sized pieces. Return the meat to the pot full of greens and allow to simmer until the liquid in the pot has evaporated—another 15 minutes or so. (Watch the pot; we don't want to burn our greens, do we?)

Adjust seasoning. Cover and keep warm on the stovetop until you're ready to assemble the dish.

Note: You can cook the turnip greens a day ahead and simply re-heat before serving.

For the Grits:

In my experience, grits don't keep too well once they're done. You can keep them in a warm oven loosely covered for up to 30 minutes before serving, but I wouldn't push it.

1½ cups stone-ground yellow corn grits
6 cups water
2 teaspoons salt
1/2 teaspoon freshly ground black pepper
1/2 cup unsalted butter
1 cup frozen yellow corn kernels
1½ cups grated sharp cheddar cheese
3/4 cup grated parmigiano reggiano cheese

In an ovenproof medium pot, bring the water to a boil and slowly whisk in the grits. You don't want any lumps, so take your time. Add the salt. Cook uncovered over medium-low heat, stirring frequently, until the grits soften and thicken up—about 45 minutes.

Add the pepper, butter, corn and cheese. Stir to combine. Simmer an additional 10 minutes or until creamy. Allow the grits to sit on the stovetop over very low heat while you cook the shrimp, or put the pot (covered) in a warm oven for up to 30 minutes.

For the Shrimp:
Fresh shrimp are best for this dish but if you have to buy them flash frozen, thaw and thoroughly dry the shrimp on paper towels before cooking. The shrimp should be cooked just before serving.

2 teaspoons Hungarian paprika (fresh)
1 teaspoon salt
1 teaspoon freshly ground black pepper
1 pound large, peeled, de-veined shrimp (tails off)
4 garlic cloves minced
2 scallions chopped, including green tops
2 tablespoons flat-leaf parsley chopped
1/4 cup peanut oil
2 tablespoons unsalted butter

Put the shrimp in a big bowl. Sprinkle in the paprika, salt and pepper. (Fresh paprika is infinitely better than the paprika in the tin you've had in the cupboard for the last two years.) Toss the shrimp to completely coat them with the spices.

Heat the oil in a large skillet over moderate heat until hot but not smoking.

Add shrimp and cook until white—2 to 3 minutes. Do not overcook.

Reduce heat to low and add garlic, scallions, parsley and butter. Allow butter to melt and combine with the oil. Toss and serve immediately.

Plating:
Spoon about a cup of the hot grits into each of four large bowls. Spoon turnip greens to one side of grits. Spoon shrimp and pan juices over the grits and serve.

This dish is way at the top of my dinner list...

Mr. Birdsong

People who know me are shocked that I've written a couple of books. They can't believe it. They know me as an average sort of guy who doesn't normally have much of interest to say. I'm really not a very interesting person.

So, they usually ask this question, "Sam, how in the world did you become an author?"

But, the other day, I got a call from my Nashville friend, Bert—a fellow I spent a lot of time with growing up in Nashville and one of my best friends. We don't keep up like we should, but in spite of our poor correspondence record, he knows me very well. Instead of asking the usual question about how I became an author, Bert asked a different question. This is how it went:

(The phone rings...)

"Hey, Sam."

"Yes," I say.

"This is Bert. Your old friend, Bert."

"Oh, hi," I say with honest delight. "It's great to hear your voice."

"I'm glad I caught you," Bert says. "You're a hard guy to track down."

And then he went on, "I'm just calling to tell you that I finally bought your books."

"Great," I say. "It's about time. You're calling to tell me that it's taken one of my best friends about a year to get around to buying my books. No wonder so few other folks are buying them."

"Well," he says. "I've bought them but I haven't read them yet."

"Bert," I say. "You've called me to tell me that you're just getting around to buying my books and that you haven't read them yet?"

"Hold on, hold on," he says. "Let me finish before you jump all over me. I have your books on my bedside table and last night I glanced over at them—stacked one on top of the other—before I turned out the light. And it occurred to me that there are a lot of words in those books."

"Yep, you're right about that," I say. "Observant as ever… "

"Well Sam, I know you as an average sort of guy who doesn't have much to say—certainly not much of interest to say. And, that makes me wonder where all those words came from. Where did all those words come from?"

That is a good question.

Now, whether you've read my books or not, and, if you've read them, whether you liked them or not, there is one thing we can all agree on: If you sit down and count the words in the three books I've written thus far, you'll find that there are a lot of words in them—something over 150,000 words. That's a lot of words. And folks who know me can't imagine where all those words came from.

To answer this fascinating question, I'm afraid I must digress... Once again, those of us interested in getting to the bottom of this very important question can be thankful that Annie is not here looking over my shoulder at the moment. She hates it when I digress.

Let's go back in time to 1957, to the neighborhood where I grew up on the outskirts of Nashville, Tennessee. My neighborhood—I take a proprietary interest in the place—ran up and down a narrow valley surrounded by low hills heavily wooded in oak, maple, tulip and sycamore trees. The road I lived on—Jocelyn Hollow Road—ran from the open end of that valley several miles to the other end and ended at the foot of a towering red clay cliff.

My neighborhood was alive with kids. I've tried to go back and count the number of us who would have been 5, 6 or 7 years old in 1957 and I stopped counting at 22—figuring that it was enough to make my point.

I was 6 years old.

In the midst of all those children, there lived one elderly man—Mr. Birdsong. Yep, that was really his name. I swear.

Mr. Birdsong was tall, thin, slightly bent forward from the middle of his back, and old. What little hair he had was white—just a few strands above each ear. He claimed that his hair had once been jet black.

Mr. Birdsong had huge ears. When we kids inquired about them, he'd tell us that he'd grown them extra large on purpose because he knew lots of old people who were hard of hearing and did not want to suffer the same fate.

His arms and hands were sort of crooked.

The old man lived in an old clapboard house painted white, with a dark green roof, dark green shutters and a big front porch with a concrete floor painted brick red. On the porch, there was a heavy wrought iron glider softened with flowery plastic-covered cushions that would rock Mr. Birdsong and at least four of us kids if we didn't move around too much.

Mr. Birdsong always wore coveralls because he had converted his one-car garage into a woodworking shop and spent most every waking hour out there crafting small pieces of furniture. He often told us stories about Mrs. Birdsong, or Ruth, who'd died a number of years before. He remarked once that it was a good thing she was dead because he would never hear the end of it if Mrs. Birdsong were there to see what he'd done to the garage.

The garage was littered with a stool project over here and a bench project over there and a lamp spindle on the lathe and a rocking chair hanging from its rockers above the work bench and pieces of lumber up in the rafters. Everything was coated in sawdust.

In one corner there was a tall wing chair covered in blue and green stripes that had seen better days. Stuffing protruded from the seat cushion and both arm rests. And just inside the door to the shop there was a small table and on the table was "The Bowl"—a great big wooden bowl that Mr. Birdsong kept chock full of individually wrapped candies.

These were no ordinary candies. The colorful wrapping on each piece concealed the nature of the candy within. No matter how hard we kids worked, we could never figure out what was inside.

Every day after school, we kids would get off the school bus in front of my house, run home, change into our play clothes and high-tail it down to Mr. Birdsong's shop where we'd find him in the middle of one of his projects. No matter what he was doing, he'd stop, wipe his hands on a really dirty rag that hung from his coveralls pocket, pick up The Bowl, seat himself in his big chair, and offer us kids a piece of candy—one piece each. Mr. Birdsong did not want to incur the wrath of our mothers.

For the longest time, we'd hover around The Bowl trying to pick out just the right piece of candy. It was hard to choose. And when finally I did choose a piece and start to open it, Mr. Birdsong would say (with slight smile on his face), "Now, Sammy, are you sure that's the piece of candy you want?" He'd plant just the smallest seed of doubt that'd send me back to The Bowl to find a better piece. Oh, what fun that was. We loved that time with Mr. Birdsong each day.

On nice days, we'd eat and run—leaving Mr. Birdsong to his projects while we kids went off to play baseball, or kick the can, or basketball, or some other game. But on rainy days or cold days, a few of us would hang out in Mr. Birdsong's shop and help him with his projects. Mr. Birdsong would give us each something to do. Jimmy liked to glue; Franny liked to sand; and I liked to oil. Rubbing walnut oil on a piece of finely sanded mahogany would bring out the grain so that you could see deep into the wood. Sometimes

we'd all stop and just marvel at what you could see if you looked closely at a piece of oiled wood.

While we worked, we kids peppered Mr. Birdsong with questions and begged him to tell us stories about Mrs. Birdsong, his twin brother Pete, and his kids—Tom, Lindsey and Noah.

He told us about meeting Ruth at a church social in his hometown of Paris, Tennessee when he was 16 years old and Ruth was just 15. Her family had just moved to town. Her dad was the new minister at the church and had brought his family to the church that Sunday afternoon to introduce them around. He told how he'd first seen Ruth as she came into the Fellowship Hall of their little Methodist church. And how he couldn't look at her, but couldn't take his eyes off of her.

We kids didn't understand that—or rather I should say, we boys didn't understand that. Franny said that she understood it and that there was nothing surprising about it at all because Mr. Birdsong, without knowing it, was looking at his future bride and in that special case anything was possible.

Mr. Birdsong just smiled when Franny said things like that. She was always saying things like that—and they made no sense to Jimmy or me. Mr. Birdsong would grin at Franny, wink, and say that one day we boys would understand... and Franny would put on her well-practiced smug look of condescending satisfaction.

Mr. Birdsong said he was smitten the first time he laid eyes on Ruth, and Franny quizzed him mercilessly about how Ruth had accomplished the smiting. What was she wearing? And how had she done her hair? And what kind of shoes was she wearing? And was she smiling? And did she ever look at Mr. Birdsong? It was clear that Franny intended to do a little smiting herself someday and wanted to be prepared.

We boys would tell Franny that she was asking Mr. Birdsong too many questions and Mr. Birdsong would stop us from teasing her and tell Franny she should ask all the questions she wanted because it gave him an opportunity to think back... and see Ruth for the first time all over again... and remember every detail about her.

He'd tell us that when he was alone in his shop or

reading the newspaper at night while he ate his dinner, he'd often think back on these times long ago, and how much he enjoyed seeing Ruth again and talking with her.

That kind of talk always baffled us kids—even Franny. How could he hear her talking if she was dead? And he'd tell us that for him she wasn't dead— that he often heard her voice and talked with her. He then said something really confusing—he said that one day we'd hear voices too. And that they'd bring great comfort to us and serve as good guides.

He told us that it had taken him several weeks to get up the nerve to talk to Ruth after he first saw her, and we'd say that couldn't be true because she was just a girl and anybody could talk to a girl anytime they wanted. And Franny would put on her smug face again and say something like, "Whenever will you boys grow up?" and then she'd ask Mr. Birdsong if he thought we boys would ever "get it."

Mr. Birdsong said he'd only gotten up the nerve to talk to Ruth when he saw her talking with another boy at church one Sunday and how that had stirred something in him that stiffened his back and walked him right over to Ruth where he stood jabbering on about things that were nonsense and how she'd smiled at him and he'd felt totally embarrassed and had rushed off because he'd made a perfect fool of himself.

Franny would say, "Poor Mr. Birdsong," while we boys were still wondering why Mr. Birdsong had rushed off.

He told us how his mom had made him go to the

Wednesday night supper at the church three days later and how Ruth was there but he couldn't bring himself to talk to her. He'd gotten in the supper line with a friend of his and hadn't noticed that Ruth had gotten in line behind him and how when he turned around and looked at her smiling at him, he'd dropped his silverware... and then dropped his plate when he reached down to recover his fork. And how he was embarrassed all over again and wished that he could just disappear. And how she'd helped him clean up the big mess he'd made and asked him if he'd sit with her when he got a fresh plate full of food.

When they sat down together on fold-up chairs in the corner of the Fellowship Hall that night, he said Ruth had started right in talking about moving to a new town and how shy she was and how difficult it was to talk to new people. She went on to say that, for some reason, she felt like Mr. Birdsong could understand and that talking with him—even though he wasn't talking at all—was easier because he understood. After that night, Mr. Birdsong said, he and Ruth were inseparable and had lived out the rest of their lives together.

Mr. Birdsong told us wonderful stories about exploring the limestone caves up in the hills above their farmhouse, about the time his twin brother Pete had gotten stuck in one of those caves late one afternoon, and how Mr. Birdsong had run all the way home to tell his mom—leaving Pete in the darkening cave all alone—and how the volunteer firemen had commandeered a neighbor's farm truck to get up an abandoned dirt road near the cave to haul in the ropes and shovels and other rescue equipment required to extricate Pete from that cave, which they did, but not until well after midnight, and how Pete was shaking so badly that they'd taken him to the hospital over in Jackson where they helped him calm down.

He told stories about his son Tom and the time he swung on a frayed rope from the rafters of the barn and, when the rope broke, how Tom went flying into the barn door and got a rusty nail in his forehead that Ruth had pulled out while Tom screamed.

He told about teaching Lindsey to drive in the church parking lot and the time she ran the truck into the flowerbed by the parking lot and nearly into the sanctuary.

And he told about Noah, when he was just 4 years old, and how he chased the milk truck down their driveway just like their dog, Rags, had done.

We loved Mr. Birdsong's stories and begged him to tell them over and over. He recounted stories about folks he'd known and told us how thinking about them and listening for their voices brought them close to him again... and how much he hoped we'd one day hear voices like he did.

* * * * *

You are probably wondering what ever happened to Mr. Birdsong.

Unfortunately, he died a few years later. Lindsey, his daughter, came to arrange the funeral and then the rest of his family showed up, and then, except for Lindsey, they all went away. A moving van arrived a couple of weeks later and took most everything out of Mr. Birdsong's house, but we kids got there in time to ask Lindsey if we could have The Bowl and she said absolutely, yes—that Mr. Birdsong was sitting up in Heaven nodding his head telling Lindsey that she should leave The Bowl for us kids.

Somehow, I inherited The Bowl. It sits on a small table beside my desk. It's full of loose change, old keys, orphaned buttons and a bunch of other stuff.

* * * * *

As I said earlier in this book, there came a time when I figured out that I wanted to do some writing in coffee shops that serve good homemade pastries. I felt like I needed a plan.

So, no matter how many times this approach has failed me in the past, I decided that I'd go study on writing. I'd get a bunch of books at my local bookstore and read them all while I drank good coffee and ate the occasional pastry.

Every day for several weeks, I got up early, swam a few slow laps at the community pool and then, feeling a little too proud of all the calories I'd burned, headed off to the bookstore, wandered to the back where they serve coffee and homemade pastries, grabbed a seat at the counter, and ordered a black drip coffee and a cinnamon bun that was surprisingly large. And then I settled into reading about writing.

The books did not seem to be much in agreement on anything except this: They all seemed to agree that a writer should write, and that keeping a regular daily writing schedule was an important thing to do. I did not feel like I was getting much in the way of specific guidance, or that sitting down to write every day was much of a plan. But I did it anyway.

The first few days were, to say the least, pretty discouraging. I pushed my feeble brain to recollect important events and the great life lessons I'd learned. I couldn't think of a single event or lesson worthy of jotting down.

After three or four days of this, I'd managed a short list of four less-than-interesting events and found myself daydreaming about them. I'd shake myself awake—disgusted with my wandering brain and lack of focus—and get myself back on the track to certain frustration.

Then one day, as I went off track again and started daydreaming about my old neighborhood and childhood friends, I scribbled mostly incoherent notes in the margin of my writing journal and occasionally stopped to outline my thoughts and organize them into a little story—making up parts to fill in the gaps. This was sort of fun and beat the hell out of serious writing.

And then I heard my neighborhood friend, Jimmy, talking in my daydream and I could talk back. And we started up a conversation and then Franny joined in and I found myself there in Mr. Birdsong's shop, oiling a piece of wood and watching the grain come to life. I could hear Mr. Birdsong's voice telling us about the voices and what a comfort they were to him and how important they'd be to us someday, too, if we'd only let ourselves hear them.

I shook myself awake again, started to lecture myself again for letting my brain go astray, but caught myself before I got too deep in the self-loathing. The voices... I was hearing the voices...

After a while it was easy. I happen to be very good at daydreaming and after some regular practice the daydreams played themselves out like short movies. They grew more vivid each day; the characters took on roles and distinct personalities; and their voices came through loud and clear. All I did... and this is the honest truth... all I did was watch the movies and take down what the voices said as fast as my two fingers could type. (I never learned to type properly. I have what one onlooker called an "interesting approach" to keyboarding.)

I found that all I had to do was find a quiet place where I could be alone with my thoughts and watch the movies in my head and listen to the voices. As Annie and I moved from Seattle to Walla Walla and built our little farmhouse way out on the prairie, our lives got quieter and quieter, and I found new locations for my daydreaming—the front porch, a small clearing down by the river where we put an old picnic table and a few beat up old chairs, my little (and I do mean "little") office in town, the Whitman College Library... the list goes on...

By now you probably appreciate that Walla Walla is, unless there is a parade in progress, a very quiet place.

* * * * *

So, there's the answer to the fascinating question about where all the words came from... or how an average sort of guy who does not normally have much to say—certainly not much of interest to say—can write down so many words and put them in books. If you hear voices, writing is an easy thing to do, but it is not the kind of thing you go around talking about in a small town.

I'm quite sure the Walla Wallans I know already think me strange enough without my wandering around telling them I hear voices...

Pulled Pork Barbeque on Corncakes

I don't even know where to start... There is a great deal to say about this dish. The most important thing to say is that you'll love it. Trust me on this one.

And don't leave the coleslaw off because you think it doesn't belong on top of the pork. It does belong... Just try it and if you don't like it, write me a nasty note. You'll feel better and I'll be able to scratch you off my list of folks I'd like to meet some day.

When I was a kid visiting the relatives in Jackson, Tennessee, we boys would be shuttled from one set of grandparents for a few days to the other set for as long as they could stand us and then off to the farm where we'd spend a few weeks with our aunt and uncle. Each of these households had its favorite barbeque shack.

At Mimi and Grandaddy's house we were treated to Moses' barbeque because it was the best pulled pork barbeque in the whole state. (There never was any mention of barbeque from other states because it wasn't worth mentioning.)

At Grandmother and Grandy's house, we'd drive with my grandfather way out into the country and pull up at a tiny little concrete block building where we'd get pulled pork barbeque from Henry. His was the best barbeque in West Tennessee. (There was no discussion of barbeque from other parts of the state because it wasn't worth discussing.)

And then, out at the farm with my aunt and uncle, Miss Mamie's cousin, Pokey, would arrive in his beat-up old truck and deliver a small, beat-up Coleman cooler packed to the lid in pulled pork barbeque.

(There never was any mention of other pulled pork barbeque.) We asked my uncle if he'd ever had Henry's barbeque or Moses' barbeque and he said, "No. Why would I want to go and try their barbeque when Pokey delivers damned good barbeque?"

Tennessee people can get territorial about their barbeque, and you should know that when a Tennessean says "barbeque," she means pulled pork barbeque. To a Tennessean, there is no other kind. And Tennesseans have learned to buy their barbeque from their favorite barbeque shack and just keep quiet about it. It's easier to avoid annoying arguments that way.

* * * * *

A few weeks ago, I was driving down Rose Street in Walla Walla and saw smoke rising from the Tumac store down the way. There were balloons everywhere tied onto farm implements of all types blowing this way and that in a fairly stiff breeze.

I'd bought a mower there... and a blanket harrow... and I'd admired some other baby boomer farmer equipment there—particularly a little tractor that looked like a lot of fun to do important farm stuff with...

So, I pulled in, followed the smoke and found that there were really nice Traeger grills on sale... Oh well, it wouldn't hurt to look... and Annie was out of town... and, well, I'd been thinking that we needed a grill out at the farm...

Mike showed me the grills and, in no time at all, I decided I was right—we did need a grill out at the farm—the one with the digital temperature monitor and the extra-large fuel hopper and the high-capacity cold smoker... I hadn't, until that moment, appreciated just how badly I needed a Traeger.

I called Annie on my cell phone... The grill was the sort of big-ticket item we'd typically talk about and think a lot about before we'd buy, so I needed to talk it over with her.

She said she'd like to see it—those were her exact words—before we bought one. She was mostly worried that it'd block our view of the mountains from the porch. (The grill is sort of big.)

So, just like she'd asked, I showed Annie a picture of it when she got home on Sunday night—handed her a brochure so she could see it—and then avoided discussion about it... and then went early on Monday morning and bought it.

I love my Traeger.

Well, you probably think that I'm going to tell you that you need to go buy a Traeger grill to make this dish... and I'll admit that slow-cooking a big fat pork butt on the Traeger for nine or ten hours is a remarkably tasty way to cook pork... but you can cook the pork butt in your oven and it'll turn out just fine.

By the way, the corncakes are fabulous.

Pulled Pork Barbeque on Corncakes
Serves 6

For the Pork:
6-pound fresh pork butt (bone-in) with skin removed
2 cups apple juice

For the Pork Rub:

1/4 cup brown sugar
2 tablespoons kosher salt
1 tablespoon freshly ground black pepper
1 tablespoon Hungarian paprika
1 tablespoon red pepper flakes
1 tablespoon freshly ground white pepper
1 tablespoon ground cumin
1 tablespoon ground coriander

For the Barbeque Sauce:

1 cup tomato catsup
1 cup cider vinegar
1/2 cup brown sugar
1½ teaspoons red pepper flakes
1 teaspoon salt
1 teaspoon freshly ground black pepper

Prepare the pork rub and coat the pork butt all over, rubbing the mixture into the meat. Leftover pork rub will keep nicely, stored in a small tin in your cupboard.

Preheat oven to 275°.

Put pork butt on a rack in a large roasting pan—fat side up. Place in oven and cook for 8 hours, basting with apple juice every hour or so. At 8 hours, check the internal temperature of the pork with a meat thermometer. Internal temperature should be about 190°.

Baste pork with barbeque sauce every 15 minutes thereafter until the internal temperature of the pork hits 200° to 210°. Remove from oven, place pork on cutting board and let the pork rest for 15 minutes.

Use one fork to hold the meat in place, and use another fork to "pull the pork" meat into chunky strips. Discard roasting pan juices, place pulled pork back in the pan; add just enough of the sauce to moisten the meat; cover the pan with aluminum foil; and return pan to oven, reducing heat to 200°. Keep pork warm while you prepare plates for serving.

For the Coleslaw:

This is difficult to admit, but I use the bagged coleslaw you can buy in any supermarket and then add just enough coleslaw dressing to moisten the slaw.

Jackie, who has tested most of the recipes in this book, jumped all over me for not giving you a coleslaw recipe. So here's Jackie's recommendation. It's real good...

4 cups shredded green cabbage
2 cups shredded purple cabbage
1 carrot shredded
1 parsnip shredded
3/4 cup Marzetti Coleslaw Dressing (or other store-bought coleslaw dressing)
1/4 cup of the barbeque sauce (see above)
1/2 teaspoon celery seeds
1/4 teaspoon freshly ground black pepper

Combine all ingredients in a large bowl and refrigerate until you're ready to serve the meal.

Feel free to do your own thing here. You just don't want your coleslaw to be at all soupy.

For the Corncakes:
1 cup all-purpose flour
2/3 cup stone ground yellow cornmeal
1 teaspoon baking powder
1 teaspoon sugar
1/4 teaspoon Hungarian paprika

1½ teaspoons salt
2 cups frozen yellow or shoe peg corn kernels
1 cup whole milk
4 tablespoons unsalted butter, melted
2 large eggs
Vegetable oil for the griddle

Pre-heat oven to 200°.

In a large bowl, mix together flour, cornmeal, baking powder, sugar, paprika, and salt. Puree 1 cup corn with milk in blender, add butter and egg and blend just until combined. Pour blended mixture into dry ingredients, add the remaining 1 cup corn, and stir until combined. Heat 2 tablespoons vegetable oil in a large cast iron skillet over medium heat. Using a ¼-cup measuring cup, pour batter into skillet and cook until bubbles appear in batter surface and bottom of corncake is golden brown. Flip corncake and cook until golden brown on the other side. Transfer the corncake to the warming oven on a cookie sheet covered loosely with foil. Repeat.

Plating
Place two corncakes on a plate.

Pile on a big helping of the barbeque. Top the barbeque with a couple of spoonfuls of the barbeque sauce. Then, top the barbeque with a couple of great big spoonfuls of the coleslaw.

I have yet to serve this to anybody who didn't rave about it.

McLeod Elementary

Dear Brad:

Sorry we missed your call. Annie and I were off on a whirlwind tour of the East Coast last week visiting Jolie and Summer.

I think Annie has probably told you that Jolie is now living in New York City and going to graduate school there. Summer is back in Charlottesville teaching first grade after a teaching stint down in Honduras. And Marshall is in her sophomore year at Central Washington University over in Ellensburg—three hours away from the farm. So, Annie can no longer conduct her midnight patrol through the house to make sure that the girls are home and tucked safely into their beds.

This means that we must periodically pack a couple of bags and get on a plane or take a road trip to check up on things. On arrival, we always find that our darling daughters are all grown up and somehow thriving without our onsite guidance. We experience great relief. And then we take the opportunity to deliver great quantities of pent up advice and wisdom.

Well, you will not believe this little coincidence.

Daughter Summer McLeod teaches at a school named "McLeod Elementary School." We don't run into the McLeod name much, so we were surprised when she told us. We've heard so many stories about her classroom that I'd often said I'd like to meet her kids. Well, as luck and constant badgering would have it, Annie and I were invited to visit Summer's classroom and have lunch with her kids during the Charlottesville part of our trek.

So, last Thursday, Annie and I showed up at McLeod Elementary in time to visit Summer's first grade classroom for about 30 seconds before we were instructed by "Ms. McLeod" to get up out of our pint-sized seats and walk slowly to the classroom door where we were to line up to go to lunch. That's when James, a three-foot-tall, six-year-old black kid with wide open brown eyes bolted from his desk under the disapproving glare of Ms. McLeod, grabbed my hand and pulled me toward the door where he announced that he was having lunch with me, and would show me to the cafeteria where he would be my self-appointed lunch guide.

We all walked single file in an almost-well-behaved line down the hall to the cafeteria where bedlam reigned. The cafeteria was full of kids—several hundred kids barely big enough to sit on the tiny little seats attached to the lunchroom tables. Very few of them were actually seated; most were on their knees so they could reach across the tables to mess with their tablemates.

It has been a very long time since I've eaten elementary school cafeteria food—42 years to be exact. One of the few things I remember about elementary school lunches is butter brickle ice cream, frozen hard inside paper cartons that never—not once—opened the way they were supposed to. By the time I'd broken into one of those little cartons, it looked like it'd taken a ride through a shredder. And, once I got to the ice cream, it was still so hard-frozen that I couldn't dig it out of the mangled paper carton without breaking the little, wooden tongue depressor-like spoon that came with the carton. I have fond memories of butter brickle ice cream, so I was looking forward to it. I just assumed that butter brickle ice cream would still be on the elementary school menu.

But James said he'd never heard of butter brickle ice cream and besides, McLeod Elementary didn't serve ice cream. He said I could have an apple instead. My heart was breaking.

James insisted that I have the chef salad—the tiniest little chef salad you've ever seen buried deep in ranch dressing—and an apple that he carefully selected for me. (Annie had told James that Mr. McLeod was on a diet and that James needed to monitor Mr. McLeod's cafeteria line ordering.) James did let me decide whether I wanted regular milk or chocolate milk, but was careful to point out that the chocolate milk was much tastier than the regular milk and had all the white milk "vite-mens" in it. So, I picked up my half pint of chocolate milk and got a high five from James who was delighted that I was a good listener, could take advice, and had managed to make a good decision pretty much on my own.

When I arrived at the table, Ms. McLeod (daughter

Summer) directed me to my chair and instructed me to sit quietly and eat my lunch and keep my hands to myself. Yes, ma'am.

Annie was already seated several stools away surrounded by Assan, Diego, Bailey and Santiago. James and Charla were sitting across the table from me. Daphne sat to my left and Robbie sat on my right.

Among my little crowd, eating did not seem to be very high on the priority list. I was peppered with questions about my name. How could I be Mr. McLeod if Summer was Ms. McLeod? And even more confusing: How could Annie be Ms. McLeod if Summer was Ms. McLeod? And why was McLeod Elementary named after us? And did we own the school? And, if so, could we please make recess a little longer?

James wanted to know if we would start serving butter brickle ice cream in our cafeteria. Even though he'd never heard of butter brickle, he seemed confident he'd like it because he'd never had any ice cream he didn't like.

And how old was I?... No, that couldn't be true. Their grandmas were younger than me.

And had I ever grounded Summer? And why? Probably for asking too many questions. Probably for talking while other people were trying to talk. Probably for chewing her food with her mouth wide open. These very good reasons had no effect on the kids' behavior but seemed solid reasons for grounding Ms. McLeod. In fact, almost any reason seemed a good reason to ground Ms. McLeod as they argued their way through a long list of the sins they felt sure Ms. McLeod had committed when she was a first grader.

And then we were on to food. What was my favorite food? And before I could reply, James said his was barbequed chicken… "No, no, no"… Daphne said he meant spicy buffalo wings… and James said "nuh-uh"… he'd said barbequed chicken and he meant what he said… and Daphne "don't know nuthin"… and then we were on to macaroni and cheese which everybody agreed is the very best food you can eat.

Next, Charla asked about Walla Walla. "Walla what?" Robbie said, while Daphne laughed out loud with her mouth open wide so we could all see the meatloaf she was chewing. "Naw, that ain't a real place," said Robbie, and James came to my defense saying it was too. He said that Ms. McLeod—the "one that's not old"—had told him already that we lived in Walla Walla and had sworn an oath on it.

And that's when Ms. McLeod—the not old one—came down to our end of the table and asked if we were exhibiting our best behavior. The question seemed to imply that we weren't and that I was more a part of the problem than the solution. And that's when we got some very clear instructions to finish up our chocolate milk and get ready to line up to go to Music after seeing our visitors, the McLeods—the old ones—to the front door.

So I gulped down the rest of my chocolate milk while Daphne reorganized the half-eaten food on my tray and started moving me (and my tray) toward the gigantic trashcan strategically positioned between tables. Then we lined up and put our hands behind our backs where they couldn't get into trouble and walked single file down the hall to the front door of the school where Ms. McLeod—the not old one—asked the kids if they had any parting words for us which they did: "Good Bye and Thanks for Coming"—almost in unison.

Annie got to say how much we'd enjoyed our visit and then it was to me. Did I have anything to say? So I invited all the kids to come with Ms. McLeod—the not old one—out to Walla Walla where we'd have a big dinner of barbequed chicken and macaroni and cheese and all the chocolate milk they could drink and butter brickle ice cream for dessert while I told them stories about all the times Ms. McLeod—the not old one—had gotten in trouble for not keeping her hands to herself, and talking while other people were trying to talk, and not sitting still in her chair, and straying out of line.

That little invitation inspired excitement and merriment in the kids to such a degree that we attracted the principal's attention. Ms. Brown came out of her office, introduced herself, thanked us for visiting, and showed us out the door while offering to deposit our name tags at the front desk for us.

Summer has since reported that our visit to her classroom was such a hit that we are not invited back unless we come at recess time on the big playground a long way from the principal's office.

Best,
SAM

Ron's Famous Firehouse Pot Roast

Ron is a friend and a winemaker. His winery is Tamarack Cellars here in Walla Walla. He makes a blended red wine called Firehouse Red that is really good—a great deal for the money. Ron uses his Firehouse Red in the following recipe. You can try making it with another wine but it just won't be the same.

When Gordy's Famous Meatballs recipe appeared in my last book, Ron went into a funk. He wanted to know why I hadn't asked him for one of his special recipes. He went on to say that Gordy's meatballs were very good. He wasn't denying that. He also admitted that the meatball recipe deserved to be written down somewhere. He was unsure whether it deserved to be in a book, though.

He said that if I wanted a great recipe definitely worthy of writing down in a book, I needed to get his famous pot roast recipe which requires three bottles of Firehouse Red—one for the recipe and two for drinking with family and friends over big plates full up with pot roast, mashed potatoes and fresh green salad.

He said that folks rave about his pot roast. And if this recipe catches on, he figures he'll be selling a lot of Firehouse Red. Ron thinks that would be a good thing.

So, I got the recipe from Ron and tried it out. This is the best pot roast I've ever eaten.

By the way, Gordy's meatballs are still the best meatballs I've ever eaten. If you want that recipe you'll have to go buy my last book, *Bottled Walla...* or borrow a copy from somebody—a practice that I do not encourage but cannot control.

Ron's Famous Firehouse Pot Roast
Serves 6

You'll need a pretty big Dutch oven with a lid.

Ingredients
1 chuck roast weighing 3 to 4 pounds
2 tablespoons vegetable oil
1/2 cup flour
1 teaspoon salt
1 teaspoon freshly ground black pepper
1 medium onion cut into ½-inch chunks
2 celery stalks cut into ½-inch pieces
2 carrots cut into ½-inch pieces
6 cloves garlic minced
1 bottle Tamarack Cellars Firehouse Red

Preheat the oven to 325°.

Mix flour, salt and pepper in a bowl and coat the chuck roast with the mixture.

Place a large, uncovered Dutch oven on the stove over medium-high heat. Add the oil and heat until the oil is shimmering but not smoking. Place the chuck roast in the Dutch oven and brown on both sides—2 to 3 minutes per side. Remove the chuck roast from the pot and set aside.

Add the onion, celery and carrots to the pot. Cook over medium heat until the onion is translucent—stirring occasionally. Add the garlic and cook an additional 30 seconds or so until the garlic is fragrant. Slowly add the bottle of Firehouse Red—stirring and scraping the bottom of the pan as you add the wine. Bring to a simmering boil. Place the chuck roast back into the Dutch oven. Put the lid on the pot and place the pot in the oven.

Cook the roast for 3 hours—turning the roast over every hour or so.

Season to taste, serve and enjoy...

Communication
Breakdown

Dear Steven:

Thank you for the "care package" you sent us. Annie has already taken all the chocolate and hidden it away. She says I do not need to be tempted by bon bons, and conceals chocolate temptations for my own good. You know as well as I do that she's addicted to the stuff and hoarding it all somewhere. She is normally a caring and sharing kind of person, but these fine qualities go into seclusion around chocolate.

I haven't found her new hiding place yet. It's just a matter of time. She moves her treasure periodically from one drawer to another trying to safeguard it. Inevitably though, I stumble on a drawer full of chocolate while looking for a screwdriver or a flashlight, and that sends her scurrying in to salvage what she can before I pocket any of it.

While we do live out in the hinterlands, we are not quite as far from civilization as your care package and waterproof matches suggest. We are only fifteen minutes from the nearest gas pump. Actually, that's not true. We are fifteen minutes from the nearest functioning gas pump. There's an old station over in Lowden that shut down for good, a long time ago. You can still read the word "Ethyl" on the side of one of the pumps where the gas hose used to hang.

Thanks for the other stuff in the package. We have managed to give most of it away. (Annie says I'm not supposed to tell you this part, but I am doing so in the interest of full and fair disclosure.)

If you haven't guessed it, we're not missing the accoutrements we left behind in the big city. Our lives are less cluttered than ever, and we now prefer it that way. Occasionally I'll think up something I "need" and then realize that a week's worth of combing the Walla Walla Valley will not find it—that I'll have to drive to Portland or Seattle to get it. And that's generally when I figure out that I don't really "need" it after all.

There is one modern age perk that has presented some hurdles. Communication with family and friends from the heart of the prairie has its own set of unique challenges. To start with, we are a little over a half mile from the nearest paved road.

When we started building our farmhouse, I called up the phone company and said we needed to get phone service at our new place. Well, the lady who answered the phone was right nice about it; she asked for a street address and said a guy named Stan would be out the next day to look things over.

So Stan showed up out at the farm, got out of his truck, and walked over to where Greg, the builder, and I were standing and watching a cement truck pour its cargo for the house foundation. Stan said, "Howdy," but didn't say another word. He pulled out a pair of binoculars and scanned the horizon. Then he turned to me and said, "You're new around here, aren't you?"

"Yep," I said. "The name's Sam."

"Well, Sam," he says. "How good are you at handling bad news?"

"About as good as most," I replied. "Why would you be asking a question like that?"

And Stan says, "Because you and me are about to have a very unpleasant conversation. I'm standing here looking off into the next state through these binoculars and I haven't seen the first sign of a telephone pole. That means that your new house is a very long way from the nearest service—wherever that is. I'm going to have to drive back into town and look at our maps and then call you and tell you something you're not going to want to hear."

"Okay," I say. "You're the phone guy. But maybe there's a buried phone line close by that you can't see with your binoculars and maybe when you look at your maps we'll all be in for a very pleasant surprise."

Stan just chuckled while shaking his head and said, "Yeah. Maybe you're right." And then he walked back to his truck, got in, and drove off down the dirt road, over the hill, and up the valley back into town.

I waited a few days. I didn't hear back from Stan like I'd expected. So, I called him up to see what was going on. He mumbled something about getting a freighter loaded in China to ferry in all the phone cable we were going to need and told me to keep my pants on, that he'd get back to me the next day for sure.

And he did. And the news wasn't what I was hoping for. In fact it was so bad that Stan talked on and on about the freighter full of phone cable, miles of trenches, big equipment, and crews called in from

every small town in southeast Washington. I kept on listening for a number—a dollar figure to quantify all this rambling—but it wasn't coming. So, I finally interrupted the unusually talkative Stan and said, "Okay Stan, let's have it. What's the bottom line?"

Things got real quiet on the other end of the line. I waited and waited and waited, and finally Stan whispered a number into the receiver that came through on my end loud and all too clear. I had to sit down. Actually, I needed to lie down. I'd never considered that phone service could possibly cost that much. And that's when Stan said, "I'll just let you think on that a while," and hung up on me.

So, that was the impetus for some education on the communication wonders of the 21st century. Without wanting to, I was starting on a mission to learn all about the availability of cell phone service in remote places, wireless Internet beamed in from faraway mountaintops, and something called "Voice Over Internet Protocol."

From the sound of things—mostly really long acronyms and hundreds of new words ending in "com"—my education wasn't going to be much fun.

My first line of inquiry focused on replacing our Seattle-based cell phone service and moving our account to a local company. So I figured I'd ask around; I'd visit the neighbors. I needed to find a company with good service out in our neck of the woods.

When I knocked on Rusty's front door he showed up with a cell phone pinned between his shoulder and his right ear. He had Betsy, his two-year-old, in one arm and a cat named Mr. Lee in the other. Through a series of winks and nods he was trying to communicate that he'd be just a minute more and handed me Betsy to entertain while he finished his conversation.

Things were looking up. I figured that I'd made the right call. I was standing in front of a guy talking on his cell phone to somebody somewhere else via some sort of invisible waves moving over the Walla Walla Valley. And I was there to ask him what cell phone service to sign up for. This was going to be easy.

That's when he started yelling, "HELLO... HELLO... HEY, MONTY... ARE YOU STILL THERE... CAN YOU HEAR ME..." and then he looked at me and Betsy and said a word that I cannot repeat, and that Betsy should not have heard. He went into a rant about his cell phone and dropped calls and "one bar" and a whole range of other subjects that needed venting. It didn't seem to be a very good time to ask about how he liked his cell phone service. After a few pleasantries, I handed Betsy back to Rusty, excused myself, and went in search of another consultant.

I figured I'd call Aida. She lives about a mile down the road, around the bend, over the river and up by the highway—a close neighbor by prairie standards. I had her cell phone number. I'd just call her up and ask her about her service. The phone rang and rang and rang some more, and then a recording of an official-sounding man talking to me from what sounded like the bottom of a muddy farm pond informed me that the cell phone customer I was trying to reach had left the service area and might never return. Well, that was enough of that; I wasn't interested in Aida's cell service if that was their definition of service.

Okay, so then I figured I'd go back and talk to the guys who were building our house. I don't know why I hadn't thought of this earlier. These guys were working on the very spot where we'd be living. They seemed to spend a lot of time leaning on various power tools while chatting on their cell phones. Maybe they could provide some guidance.

Jim said I shouldn't get the service he had. It only worked if he went into the port-o-toilet, closed the door and stood facing the plastic urinal in the corner. Ray said his phone only worked if he waited for a south wind, stood out by the well and leaned slightly into the breeze. Mike said he had the best luck if he walked over to the big pile of basalt stone that they were going to use to build our fireplace and chimney, held his phone way up in the air until it "acquired a signal," and then carefully lowered it back to chest height and dialed before the fragile signal evaporated.

Cell phones did not seem to be the answer.

A few days later, I went into town to do some writing and eat a bowl of soup at Merchants where Bob, the owner, listened to my sad story and asked if I'd considered Internet telephony. Not only had I never thought of it; I'd never heard of it. He said I should check into the availability of wireless Internet service out near our new place and, if we could get it, then check into one of the new "Voice Over Internet Protocol" phone services. He suggested I start with John.

I'll have to say that I was skeptical; but I thought back to my conversation with Stan and the exceptionally large number he'd whispered into the phone—the one that had prompted a brief dizzy spell. That got me going again.

So I called John. He asked a bunch of questions and said that, like Stan, he'd need to meet me out at the building site—that everything hinged on whether we had "line of sight" to their Internet service tower. I hadn't remembered seeing any towers out our way unless of course he was referring to the huge windmills way off on the ridge well to the south of us. But, hey, if John was willing to come out and help me see an otherwise well-hidden communications tower, who was I to stand in his way?

That afternoon, I met John at the end of our soon-to-be driveway. We forded the irrigation ditch and drove the half mile to the big hole in the ground that was becoming our new home. John liked the location and admired the incredible views. He got his binoculars out of his truck and scanned the tops of the Horse Heaven Hills about 15 miles away. There he apparently saw something that I couldn't see with my naked eyes. He handed me his binoculars and pointed me slightly southeast to a spot way off in the distance. With the binoculars you could barely make out what looked like a flagpole that'd fallen into disuse.

"You're in luck," says John. "We can put a receiver down here on the side of your barn when you get it built. And we'll point the receiver at that tower. And we'll run a line from the barn under the driveway and up through the house foundation into the attic. And then we'll hook that line into a wireless router and turn it all on. And after we play with your computer for a while, you'll be able to wander around out here in your underwear and email anybody in the world, anywhere, any time. And you'll be all set up to put in an Internet phone."

This was sounding good… and too far-fetched to be true. "So, you're telling me that what looks like a flag-pole way off across the valley and up that ridge over in the next state is going to send and receive my email and anything else I want to find on the Internet while I sit out on the porch typing away on my laptop listen-ing to the coyotes howl?" I asked.

"Yep, that's right," he says.

Wow.

And sure enough, when we got the barn built and the farmhouse attic enclosed, a guy named Andy showed up in his truck and hooked what looked like a large din-ner plate up on the side of the barn. I didn't see what all happened after that. I'm sure there were lots of wires and other electronic gadgetry involved. When I arrived back out at our new place the next day—a Saturday—to survey the progress, I was greeted by a fairly stiff breeze and a big red-tailed hawk squawking as it rode the wind down the river below the house. The construc-tion site was eerily quiet.

I didn't know whether we had the Internet service or

not, so I figured I'd just fire up my computer and give it a try. I grabbed a short ladder from inside the unfinished house, pulled it out onto what would, someday, be our front porch, perched myself on the top step and opened my laptop.

I hit the "on" button and crossed my fingers. Lo and behold, my computer came to life and informed me that it had detected a passably strong wireless connection named "McLeodCom" and was taking the liberty of hooking up to it—no error messages, no prompts to "try again," no pain, no suffering, no swearing. It was magic.

Cautiously (not wanting to disturb the good karma), I typed out a short email to my brother, Larry, who was likely sitting in front of his computer in Sao Paulo, Brazil. If I was going to send a test email, I might as well send one way off to another hemisphere and give this wireless service a real test. I hit the "send" button pretty hard hoping to give my email an extra boost. After all, it had a long way to go and nothing to support it on its flight from the porch to that tower off on the edge of good vision.

Then I waited... about 30 seconds... before getting a message back that said, "Hi... What's up?"

Wow.

Now, there's a lot more stuff that I had to discover and get confused about before we got to the point where I plugged Annie's old "princess" phone into the wall outlet in our brand new farmhouse. But Annie is here looking over my shoulder saying that this is the longest and ramblingest letter I've ever written and that you're bound to be nodding off by now. So, I'm going to give you the short version of the story.

Annie and I are a little old-fashioned and not very comfortable with the idea of sitting in front of a computer and just talking off into the ether without seeing the thing that's catching our words and sending them on. Well, this amused Trent, the electrician, to no end, but he humored us and put a regular phone outlet by Annie's desk that he somehow hooked up to the Internet gear hidden away in the attic. And, as I was saying before Annie started hovering over my shoulder, I plugged in that "princess" phone and heard a regular dial tone. Annie, so excited that she had to press her knees hard together, dialed her mom who answered her phone in Virginia and said she could hear us—and we could hear her. She sounded like she was next door.

Wow.

It took a few exaggerated hand gestures from me before Annie comprehended that she did not have to yell into the receiver to push her words along. We could talk in a normal voice and communicate with anybody on the planet and we could dial them up on a real phone. Annie was, all of a sudden, feeling much better about her new life as a pioneer woman.

So, now Annie has an upgraded stash of chocolate somewhere, and our lives are less cluttered, and we can both communicate with other human beings in magical ways that still leave me wondering about the people out there somewhere who think up these things. Wow.

Best,
SAM

Cold Asparagus Soup

Asparagus harvest begins in April in Walla Walla. And when the asparagus comes in, it comes in 10-pound bags—just picked and very tender. We eat asparagus almost every day from late April through early June. So, I've had to learn several hundred new ways to prepare this delicacy. My two favorites are asparagus tempura and a very easy cold asparagus soup.

Here's the soup recipe—simple and delicious. Served the "right way" in large white soup bowls garnished with crisscrossed sprigs of chive and a sprinkling of freshly grated nutmeg, it'll look like you know what you're doing.

I used to snip the tough ends off the asparagus with kitchen shears. A few days ago, a neighbor down Detour Road showed me, standing at the edge of a big field full of the fast-growing spears, how to snap the woody ends off. Hold an asparagus spear about midway up the stalk with one hand and the woody end with the other and just bend the stalk until the woody end snaps off—right where you want it to. After a little practice, even I can do this.

It'd be nice if you could use Walla Walla Sweet Onions in this recipe. As the asparagus comes in, we're just starting to get the first of the Walla Walla spring onions. So, if you live here in Walla Walla or nearby, and can get your hands on the spring onions, you'll want to use the tender bulbs in this recipe.

But if you can't get the Walla Walla spring onions, an inferior sweet onion from somewhere else will have to do.

You can make this soup a couple of days ahead and keep refrigerated until you're ready to serve.

Cold Asparagus Soup
Serves 6

Ingredients
4 tablespoons unsalted butter
2 pounds asparagus spears—cleaned, woody ends removed and cut into 1 to 2-inch pieces
1 medium sweet onion—chopped
3/4 cup dry white wine
2 cups low-sodium, low-fat chicken stock
Salt and freshly ground black pepper to taste
1/2 cup sour cream
Fresh chive sprigs
Freshly grated nutmeg

In a large soup pot, melt the butter and add the onion and asparagus. Cook the onion and asparagus over medium heat until the onion is translucent—5 minutes. Add the wine, bring to a simmer, and continue to simmer uncovered 1 to 2 minutes. Then add the chicken stock, bring back to a simmer, and simmer uncovered over medium-low heat for 20 minutes or so—until the asparagus is very tender.

Allow to cool for 10 to 15 minutes before moving on to the next step.

Puree small batches in a blender until very smooth and creamy. WARNING: Be careful to pulse each batch briefly several times, holding the blender top on securely with a kitchen-towel protected hand, until the pressure of the released heat inside the blender subsides. You do not want this soup on the ceiling of your kitchen—believe me, I know.

Cold Asparagus Soup

If you snapped the woody ends off of your asparagus before cooking, you shouldn't have to strain out solids, but you can if you want to.

Salt and pepper to taste.

Spoon the sour cream into a small mixing bowl. Add 1/2 cup of the warm soup and whisk until smooth. Then add to the soup and stir to combine. The soup should be smooth and creamy.

Refrigerate the soup for several hours until well chilled.

Serve in soup bowls, garnished with sprigs of chive and a dusting of fresh nutmeg.

The Meaning of A

E ver since I wrote my last book, *Bottled Walla*, folks have pestered me about a preamble to one of the stories in the book. There was a brief reference to one of my college professors and a lesson he taught me about "the meaning of A." Well, here is the answer to that burning question. I don't know that it'll mean as much to you as it did to me, but it was a great lesson to me.

* * * * *

As I approached the midpoint of my last year of college, I was forced to reckon with the fact that my grades needed some sprucing up—okay, well, a lot of sprucing up.

I was taking a yearlong music seminar from Professor Mead—Chair of the Music Department at the University of Virginia. His friends call him "Boots."

There were four of us students—Mark, Joe, Gordon and me. We were not musicians, but we enjoyed learning about the music, the composers, and ways of hearing the music that gave it life. We also enjoyed Mr. Mead, his wife, Sally and the animal menagerie that roamed their home.

They made an interesting pair—Boots and Sally. Mr. Mead always wore a tweedy sport coat and a bowtie from his extensive bowtie collection; he wore professorial glasses; he played Bach and Brahms; and he spoke with a noticeable Virginia accent. He took an obvious, almost paternal, interest in his students and his students loved him. They still do.

Mrs. Mead loved animals. She ran the local Society for the Prevention of Cruelty to Animals and used her home to manage animal overflow and shelter the permanently disabled creatures that came her way. Sally was a whisper of a woman most often seen running around the SPCA or her house in her tennis shoes, wearing rubber gloves to facilitate the cleaning of soiled cages. She could also throw a mean cocktail party.

Dogs roamed the Mead's home; an injured owl was a permanent resident of the large birdcage in the corner of the dining room; a big, fat raccoon wandered around the place harassing the dogs whenever he escaped from his cage in the kitchen; and an abandoned fawn nibbled on the shrubbery in the back yard. It was an interesting place.

Our seminar met weekly at the Mead's home where Mr. Mead entertained us on a beautiful grand piano in the living room. Between seminar meetings, we'd listen to several pieces of recorded music, then gather at the Mead's to talk about the music and listen to Mr. Mead play.

At 5:30pm, Mrs. Mead would appear at the living room door to rescue us from excessive edification.

Invariably she'd suggest we students stay for a drink or two. And being young gentlemen, we were not about to disappoint the lady of the house.

In October of that academic year, I asked Mr. Mead a very important question: How was he going to grade our seminar performance—a paper? an exam? both? neither? In short, I needed an "A"; what did I need to do to get an "A" in the class?

He just smiled and said he'd have to think about it. I asked again in November and he smiled and said he was still thinking about it. I asked again in December and he smiled and said he hadn't forgotten my question and was still thinking about it. This unsatisfactory pattern continued well into March and I'm sure he watched my discomfort rise with amusement. I needed to get an "A" and the sooner the better.

So, finally, in early April he called me into his office—full of books and music and papers. He asked me how I felt about the seminar, whether I'd enjoyed it, whether I'd learned anything from it, and how I judged my own performance. I'm quite sure I fumbled the answer. But, as usual, he just smiled and listened and then he answered my longstanding question—he wanted me to write a paper on "The Meaning of A."

I started to ask a slew of questions about what that meant, what he wanted, when he wanted it... but he just raised his hand to stop me and said go away, think about it, and write your paper. So, I did.

Now the shoe was on the other foot. Each week, Mr. Mead asked me how the paper was coming, what I was writing about, and what I was learning. And each week I'd just smile and answer that I was thinking about it and would get back to him. In truth, I did spend a lot of time at first trying to figure out what he wanted—a couple of weeks in fact. It took me a while to understand that it wasn't what *he* wanted or thought that mattered—that he was trying to get me to think about excellence or "the meaning of A"—what I wanted to learn, and what an "A" meant to me.

He will remember that I wrote about a piece of music called "Pictures at an Exhibition," written by a Russian composer named Modest Mussorgsky. In my paper, I compared an orchestral version of the work with a rock version performed by a popular rock band called Emerson, Lake and Palmer. In the course of writing the paper, I had to ask myself questions like, "Which interpretation is better?" and "How would anybody know?" and "Who gets to decide?"

As Mr. Mead expected, all of this musing led me to the lesson that, at the end of the day, a given performance is evaluated differently by each of us, and that, while listening to the response of the audience and his critics, the performer must learn to evaluate his own performance and be happy with it or not.

So, yes, he'd asked me to write a paper. And, yes, he'd give me a grade. And, yes, he'd critique my work. But he hoped that I'd learn not to care so much about the criticism of others and to care a great deal more about my own evaluation of my performances in this life. When I've been smart enough to remember the lesson, it has served me well.

✻ ✻ ✻ ✻ ✻

A few weeks ago I visited Charlottesville, spent a wonderful afternoon with Summer and her first graders and then, because Summer was headed to a bridal shower thrown by a bunch of her girlfriends, I had a free night and a chance to spend some time with Mr. Mead. We had a superb meal at a beautiful little restaurant, L'Etoile, and several hours to talk—just the two of us. It was a glorious evening—one that I'll never forget. I hope that we'll be able to do it again.

Mr. Mead is still interested in his students, even us old ones. And we still love him. Thank you, my teacher and friend, for all of the lessons, especially the "meaning of A."

Best,
SAM

Talkin' to Jesus

Every summer when I was a boy, my mother carted us kids off to Jackson, Tennessee to visit the relatives... for as long as they'd take us. Chasing after five young boys 11 months of the year was enough to create a willingness in my mother to give us up for a while.

Jackson used to be a very small, rural farm town in West Tennessee. In recent years, the town has grown dramatically. But back when I was a kid, it was a pretty sleepy little place surrounded by cotton fields, grazing cows and small plots of tobacco.

The drive from Nashville to Jackson was a long one—going on two hours. It seemed interminable to us kids. Proper provisioning for the trek was therefore important. Mom would fill up one cooler with Nehi orange sodas and another with tuna salad sandwiches, deviled eggs, sweet pickles, chips and Oreo cookies for dessert.

We traveled in a lime green 1960 Ford station wagon with fake wood siding. After the car was loaded to overflowing, we'd wave goodbye to Dad and strike off down the highway bound for a few weeks of country living.

About halfway along in our journey, Mom would pull over at a roadside picnic table on the east end of the Tennessee River Bridge—the same spot every year. We boys knew the place well. We'd pile out of the car and run straight to the water's edge where we'd attempt to skip rocks off the river's chocolate brown surface while Mom laid out our picnic lunch.

Our tuna salad sandwiches came on white bread with the crusts cut off. (We boys did not care for bread crusts.) The sandwiches were tucked away in wax paper bags and were cold from riding on ice in the cooler. Nehi orange soda went pretty well with a cold tuna salad sandwich. The Oreo cookies were just fine right by themselves.

The feeding frenzy over, we were off again—over the Tennessee River Bridge into West Tennessee and then through endless fields of cotton, soybeans and corn to the parsonage where Grandmother and Grandy—my Mom's parents—lived. My grandfather was a Methodist minister. Grandmother was a grandmother… and a good one at that.

Long before we arrived, Grandmother had her oatmeal cookies stacked up in a big tin on the kitchen table and her refrigerator stocked with frothy, very cold milk. We boys knew the drill. As soon as we pulled into the parsonage driveway, we started jockeying for position, and once parked, made a beeline from the car to the back door—gateway to the cookies.

I'm quite sure my Mom and Grandmother spent a great deal of time unloading the car and putting away our duffel bags, but I have no recollection of it.

After a short visit with Grandmother, Mom would

kiss us each goodbye and deliver a litany of instructions, which mostly boiled down to "don't torture the relatives and don't wipe your nose with the back of your hand."

Then she'd drive off looking sad but waving vigorously and probably smiling inside about all the things she was going to do on her extended vacation from mothering.

Grandmother and Grandy could deal with us for two, maybe three, days before they ran out of steam and shuttled us off to Mimi and Grandaddy's house, our grandparents on my father's side of the family. We'd tag along with Grandaddy to his shop where he made baseball bats for us on his lathe while Mimi cooked up huge quantities of food for our supper and tried to restore order in their little house. Like the other grandparents, they'd try to keep up with us for a few days before carting us off to the farm—the farm where our Aunt Irma and Uncle Pete would take us in for several weeks.

My aunt and uncle were brave and patient people—personality traits that were easier to pull off in a place where there was an inexhaustible supply of adventures that kept us boys mostly off in the back forty, well away from the adults. We were easier to deal with at great distance.

* * * * *

The farm was a Civil War survivor. My aunt told us eye-popping stories about how my uncle's grandparents had opened up the farmhouse to be used as an infirmary for the Confederate Army, and how a night-time raid by Yankees had left bullet holes in two of the upstairs doors—holes big enough that you could stick your index finger through them. Faded photos in wooden frames decorated the walls—stern-looking men wearing the uniform of the Confederacy and primly proper women in dark dresses buttoned up to the chin. My aunt could tell you the place of everyone of those folks in my uncle's family history and everything you'd ever want to know about each of them. There was a locked glass case full of Confederate rifles, swords and medals at the far end of the upstairs hallway.

The farmhouse was a two-story white clapboard box with a double-decker front porch that ran across its front and around its east corner to the kitchen door. Porch ceiling fans turned day and night.

The porch on the main floor featured two porch swings, lush potted ferns and an eclectic assortment of rocking chairs and small tables (for setting your lemonade glass on). The bead-boarded porch ceilings were painted light blue to discourage wasps from constructing their nests up there. A big plastic tub of string beans waiting to be strung and snapped sat on one of the rocker seats.

Inside the house there was a living room that we never hardly saw, a dining room crowded by a long harvest table where we took our noon meal, and a grand old kitchen that contained a wood-fired stove and a breakfast table with seating for ten.

Behind the kitchen was Mamie's room—a tiny self-contained apartment that opened onto the kitchen porch—a place that looked like it had been tacked onto the house as an afterthought. I'll get to Mamie a little further on in this story. There's only the upstairs of the farmhouse and several hundred acres to describe before we get to Mamie.

Upstairs were the bedrooms—one huge room where my aunt and uncle slept and two bedrooms across the hall where we boys were housed. One of our bedrooms opened out onto the upstairs porch where there were a couple of steel-framed beds that provided open-air comfort on the hottest, most humid of summer nights. If we boys promised not to hang over the balcony railing, we were permitted to drag our blankets and pillows out onto the porch where we could set up camp for the night.

Only one of us ever leaned too far out over the porch railing and fell off that balcony porch. It was brother Larry. He fell into the sticker bushes headfirst but escaped the incident without dying or losing any limbs. That was the last time any of us played on the railing.

There were animals everywhere. A menagerie of cats and dogs roamed the porches and the yard in front of the house. Cats lived in the barn and under the back porch; dogs rolled in the dusty bare spots out by the chicken coop; chickens pecked their way around the base of the gargantuan oak tree that shaded the front of the house; and a cocky rooster strutted about, menacing everything in sight. We boys learned to steer clear of him.

There were pigs down by the barn. The baby pigs were always escaping from the pen. It was our job to chase them down and return them to their mother. A Shetland pony that was too wild to ride munched on grass out in the pasture beyond the barn. There was a small pond on the far side of the pasture that was brimming over in sunfish, bass and snapping turtles. And beyond the pond there was a dense forest of hardwoods and southern pine where you could build a respectable fort out of deadfall and mud bricks.

Speaking of ponds and mud, I forgot to tell you that there was a showerhead and a pull chain on a tall post just outside the kitchen porch door. That's where we boys were instructed to strip down each evening after we'd been called in for supper—leaving our filthy clothes in a heap on the ground. We were required to scrub ourselves raw before we were allowed to run naked through the kitchen and up the stairs to find some clean clothes to put on.

* * * * *

Finally we are getting to the main character of this long-winded tale. Her name was Mamie—an old black woman who lived with my aunt and uncle and who was as much a member of the family as any blood relative. Mamie was in charge of us boys while we were visiting at the farm. Actually, Mamie was pretty much in charge of the whole farm. We called her our summer mother.

I can't tell you where Mamie came from, or how she got to the farm or much about her family. I only met one of her relations—a cousin named Pokey who drove a wreck of a truck that he complained about more than he drove. Pokey came around pretty regularly to see Mamie. He sometimes brought along barbeque in a red Coleman cooler. But he was always yelling at that truck and my uncle was forever out there in the yard with Pokey trying to get the thing running. Mamie said that truck labored under the "devil's own curse" and that's why it "warn't never gonna do right." She could get a little put out with Pokey and his truck.

Another thing I don't know is how old Mamie was. But she was old. She looked old and talked about her "ol' bones" whenever she got up out of her rocking chair. She had what she called an "ol' woman crew cut" of tiny white curls all over her head. She wore clip-on pearl earrings that she fiddled with constantly. Her eyes were dark brown and half sunk into a face of mostly wrinkles. But you could still see Mamie's dimples; she could point them out to you; and she was always saying that I must be related to her because we both had dimples. I liked the idea of being related to Mamie.

The skin on her arms hung loose from her thin bones. There were deep folds of crusty skin where her elbows were supposed to be. She looked frail but wasn't; she could grab an out-of-control boy and jerk him to a halt just as easily as she could carry a gigantic pot of boiling potatoes from the stove to the sink—just as easily as she could chase down a chicken and lop off its head before the poor thing had any idea that it was "boun' for Heaven above, Amen." Mamie was a kind, gentle, happy soul most of the time; but you did not mess with Mamie; she could be scary when she got mad.

Mamie wore her gray work dress every day and protected it from abuse with a full apron covered in small blue flowers. She wore support-type leather shoes sometimes, but went barefoot the rest of the time. Whenever we boys sat out on the porch with my aunt and Mamie to shell beans, or string beans, or snap beans, Mamie would kick off those shoes and wiggle her toes saying that those "po' toes was sufferin' in them shoes" and that shoes "was the devil's own curse laid on ol' women." My aunt would smile and tell us boys to keep our shoes on—when we got to be Mamie's age we could run around the farm barefoot, but not before.

My aunt and Mamie had a very interesting relationship. Mamie called my aunt "Miss Irma" even though my aunt was married; and my aunt called Mamie "Miss Mamie." They were very formal that way. Mamie called it being respectful. When we asked if we were supposed to call her Miss Mamie to be respectful, she said, "Lawd, no, chil'ern. You jus' call me Mamie and we be jus' fine and happy."

Sometimes we'd hear Mamie being bossy to our aunt: "Miss Irma, you go on an' git outta this here kitchen and outta my way." And Mamie would start waving her hands out in front of her like she was going to sweep my aunt out of that kitchen. And they'd both laugh and go on about their business.

And sometimes she'd boss our uncle: "Mr. Pete, git yo'self back out on that porch in them mud boots and don't you dare be trackin' that mud in my kitchen." And Uncle Pete would go back out onto the porch and take off his boots.

MAR • 60

It was clear to us boys that Mamie owned the kitchen.

Another thing about Mamie: She sang while she worked... as long as nobody else was around.

Every morning we'd wake up to Mamie's singing in the kitchen while she prepared our breakfast. My aunt was already out in the garden collecting vegetables for lunch. My uncle was off on his tractor very early, as usual. And Mamie thought we boys were sleeping... but we weren't. We'd lie in our beds quiet as we could be and listen to her singing about swinging low, and the angel on her shoulder, and going home to Jesus.

One day, I surprised Mamie in the kitchen and asked her what she was singing.

She said, "Lawd, honey, I warn't singin'; I's jus' talkin' to Jesus."

And you know what? I believed her. I still believe her.

Mamie knew a lot of stuff. She taught us how to bait a hook with an earthworm and how to catch the huge grasshoppers hopping around in the wheat field in front of the house. She showed us how to hook those grasshoppers and float them out on the farm pond where big sunfish could pounce on them. She knew how to clean those fish, roll them in flour and fry them up for our breakfast. Mamie claimed that the fish we caught out of the pond each summer made the best breakfast anybody had ever thought up.

Mamie knew where the devil was at all times. On a walk back from the pond one morning with a stringer full of brightly colored sunfish, Randy spied a black snake slithering across the path ahead and pointed it out to the rest of us. Mamie jumped about ten feet backward, ran through the barn gate and climbed up on an abandoned pig shed. She stood up there yelling for us boys to climb up beside her "quick as sparks so's the devil cain't git us," because that black snake was "a incarnation of the devil hisself."

As I mentioned, Mamie could get mad. It didn't happen often, but when it happened, we boys were struck dumb with fear. Other than those scary times, Mamie was always happy. I don't think I ever saw her sad or moaning about anything.

I remember running into the farm kitchen once to alert Mamie to the fact that brother Gary was missing. The rest of us had been so engrossed in tormenting a hive of ground-dwelling bees that we hadn't noticed that Gary had wandered off. As I burst through the kitchen porch door, there was Gary sitting in Mamie's lap, tears running out of his eyes.

I asked what was wrong and Mamie said that Gary was feeling a little blue—just a touch sad because he was homesick. That got us off on a discussion about homesickness and somewhere in the middle of all that talk I asked Mamie if she ever got sad. I couldn't imagine Mamie sad.

"Sometimes... sometimes I's sad... but I's never sad for long," Mamie said.

"Are you ever homesick?" I asked.

"No, chile. I's home. Ain't no reason for ol' Mamie to be homesick."

"So, what makes you sad, Mamie?" I pressed.

"Lawd, chile, ain't nothing make me sad. Nuthin' ever *make* a body sad. A person get to decide that. If you sad, or mad, or whatever, it's 'cuz you choose to be. It be your choice. Don' never forget that."

* * * * *

One Sunday each year while we boys were visiting the farm, we'd get to go with Mamie to her church—the black church. It was fun. It wasn't anything like the white church.

When we went to the white church, my aunt would make us sit in the front row because there was no pew in front of us to kick at during the service. The white church was a solemn sort of place. There wasn't much excitement unless the stiff-legged altar boy threatened to set fire to something other than the candles. That seemed to happen more often than the organist might have liked. She was forever looking up from the organ music, out over her glasses, and frowning at him.

Otherwise, the white church was stern-looking choir members singing serious hymns from the pages of the official Baptist hymnal; a dour-looking preacher making a sermon on finding joy in Christ; and old ladies everywhere to smile at after church as we made the long trek from the front of the church all the way back to the massive church doors and freedom.

We did not care much for the white church. Unfortunately, my aunt wasn't terribly interested in whether we liked it or not. We were going... whether we liked it or not.

But like I said, on one of the Sundays while we were at the farm each summer, Mamie would take us to the black church. Pokey would pick us up in his truck and squeeze us boys into the smallest rear seat you've ever seen—really just an open space behind the two seats up front. Pokey would help Mamie, who was carrying a huge plate full of peanut butter cookies, into the passenger seat and then climb in behind the wheel. He didn't have to start the truck up because he'd never turned it off. Mamie saw to that. She had carefully instructed Pokey on when to pick us up (even though he already knew) and had warned him to leave the truck running while we all piled in. She'd tell us boys that she'd rather spend some time with Jesus than look at Pokey's rear end while his head was stuck up under the hood of that truck trying to get it started again.

The black church was a tiny affair way off the highway down a road that was more potholes than pavement. We parked under the trees right next to the whitewashed concrete block church and wandered through the tall weeds to the front door. Reverend Johnson was the pastor and made over us boys like we were his own. He gave us each a peppermint from his pocket while Mamie pretended to look the other way.

Folks inside the church laughed and talked so loud that our ears would ring. The ladies pinched our cheeks and the men knuckled our crew-cut heads. There were black kids everywhere chasing each other and having a gay time. It was a lively place.

But that was just the start. After a while, Reverend Johnson would wander down the aisle toward the front of that little church shaking hands with everybody now seated in pews and the din would peter away into silence. Reverend Johnson would then stand at the front of the church, raise both of his big hands, and make a prayer to Jesus while we all sat quiet as we could be. He was praying for Jesus to come to our little church and save us all from the ways of the devil.

I had to see this.

Right after the prayer, some church ladies strolled up and down the main aisle handing out cardboard fans with a church saying on one side and a picture of Jesus on the other side while the Reverend Johnson made some little joke about keeping cool with Jesus. We laughed politely. We boys loved those fans and fanned ourselves vigorously all through the service.

Next came a hymn that the small choir would start. There was no organ—just the voices of the three or four women and the two men in the choir. The song started off slow but built toward a crescendo that had us all swaying in our seats and some folks clapping along. Unlike the white church, this was a church where swaying in your seat was encouraged.

Reverend Johnson stepped into the pulpit as the hymn hit its high point and ended abruptly. He started in on his sermon nice and slow with a soft voice. We boys knew what was coming. It was like feeling the growing rumble of a freight train under foot long before the train comes barreling down on you. It was exciting.

Ever so slowly, the Reverend's voice picked up in depth and decibel level. Folks behind us started what Mamie called the "amen-ing." Reverend Johnson belted out a sentence about Jesus coming—that in his mind's eye he could see Jesus now walking down the road toward our little church to gather up His children—and everybody, including us boys, said "Amen."

And then the Reverend belted out another vision of Jesus nearing the church and seeing the cars and trucks of His children parked under the shade trees—and everybody said, a little louder this time, "Amen." And then Reverend Johnson raised his hands up high again and shut his eyes tight and said even louder that he could see our sweet Jesus stepping up to the door of the church preparing Himself to enter and greet all His children.

The choir erupted and launched into a spiritual that

everybody, except us boys, knew by heart, and the crowd joined in the singing as the Reverend Johnson strode toward the door of the church, shaking hands with the men as he went and hugging the overjoyed ladies. He was going to let our Lord Jesus in.

Well, I'm here to tell you that the place went crazy. Folks were singing themselves hoarse and screaming out their amens. Ultra-large women in high heels danced down the aisle to greet Jesus. Kids stood up in the pew seats to get a better view as the Reverend opened the doors to the church—opened them wide so the invisible presence of Jesus could accompany him back down the aisle to the front of the church as a couple of parishioners passed out from the excitement of it all and had to be laid out on pews until they could recover.

Oh my, what fun it was—singing, clapping, dancing on the pew seats and watching the show as that little church rocked on its foundation.

White people did not know what they were missing.

* * * * *

On one of those trips to the farm, I remember asking Mamie why she couldn't come to the white church with us. She shook her head and said it "warn't nuthin' worth worryin' over"—that "we'd all end up in the same church some day... on that day when our sweet Jesus came callin' us to Heaven."

Amen...

135

Coco's Pickled Shrimp

My mother used to make pickled shrimp for her New Year's Eve party. We boys were warned that the pickled shrimp were for guests and we were not to pilfer any of them before the guests arrived. Just before the party started, we were each permitted one shrimp, and my mother promised that there'd be leftovers for us if we behaved ourselves.

Well, one year there were no leftovers and we boys learned a valuable lesson.

From that day forward, anytime our parents had a cocktail party, we'd show up for the one shrimp we were offered pre-party and then hover around the shrimp bowl during the party along with everybody else. We'd allow the ladies to pinch our cheeks; we'd shake hands with the men and stand around and smile while everybody talked about how much we'd grown and how handsome we were... and we'd accept shrimp offered by our many admirers.

You will love these!

Coco's Pickled Shrimp
Serves 25 guests as an appetizer

For the Shrimp:
2½ pounds large fresh shrimp
1/2 cup celery tops
1/4 cup pickling spices
3 teaspoons salt
2 cups sliced onions
7 bay leaves

For the Marinade:

3/4 cup white vinegar
1½ cups vegetable oil
2½ tablespoons capers
2½ teaspoons celery seed
1½ teaspoons salt
1/8 teaspoon hot sauce (Tabasco)
And a box of multi-colored toothpicks for serving

Place the shrimp, celery tops, pickling spices and salt in a large pot of boiling water and cook the shrimp until they are just cooked through—2 to 3 minutes. Do not overcook. Drain the shrimp in a colander, cool under cold running water, remove shells and tails and de-vein.

Place a layer of onions in the bottom of a large, fancy, glass bowl. Then a layer of shrimp. Then a layer of onions, etc. Continue layering until you've used up all the shrimp and onions. Insert the bay leaves to distribute them evenly among the shrimp.

Combine the marinade ingredients and stir well. Pour the marinade over the shrimp. Cover the bowl. Chill for at least 48 hours before serving.

That's the hard part—waiting 48 hours before serving. Delayed gratification is something I deal with most every day—but it's worth the wait.

Jim

He approached me at the corner of the parking lot where I'd just paid the machine for a day's worth of downtown Seattle real estate.

He struggled... bobbed his head... frustrated... but finally stuttered out, "dadadadadada-da-lar."

He relaxed, exhausted by the effort.

His baseball cap—one that had, at some point in its distant past, been lime green and had sported a logo—was badly faded, logo-less and mostly dirt brown and oily black.

His greasy gray hair hung down from under the brim of his hat in long, curly strings that irritated his eyes. Dull gray irises bulged from crimson eyeballs. A matted, badly soiled gray beard and mustache hid the tip of his purple nose and his mouth.

The rest of him was worse.

I walked on by...

I am not a very sympathetic guy. Empathy is not my strong suit. I tend to believe that the less fortunate among us should "buck up," make better choices and make something of the one life they know they have to live.

I can be dismissive of the bums that panhandle their

way down our streets. They make me uncomfortable. They're dirty... and a little scary... and often smell bad... and sometimes yell incoherently. I don't like to be around human beings like that.

I am—sometimes—not a very nice person. I walked on by... to the next corner where I stood waiting for the light to change.

Much to my annoyance, I heard one of the voices—the ones that are only supposed to speak to me when I'm in a quiet place for a long time, not trying to hear them, drinking a hot cup of coffee, and occasionally eating a pastry. I was not in a quiet place; downtown Seattle is not a quiet place.

The voice said, "Bad boy, Sam. That was not nice—not nice at all—and I'm not very happy with you at the moment. That guy could use a little compassion, a kind word, and maybe a good meal."

My own personal, guilt-whispering, nagging voice that interferes with my mostly blissful, detached existence on this planet was at it again. I hate it when that happens.

The light changed. I stepped off the curb and then said, "For God's sake," under my breath and turned around. There he was... standing right behind me. Of all the folks who'd walked by him that day—stepping out of the imaginary lane we all walk down a sidewalk to dodge this dirty human's aura—I was the one he'd chosen to follow.

"Why me?" I mumbled.

He stood there. He glanced at the air to the left of my head but he wouldn't look at me. He didn't try to speak. I put my hand in my pocket and searched with my fingertips to locate some change. His eyes locked onto my pocket.

And the voice said, "C'mon, Sam. That's a little too easy isn't it? How about giving a little more?"

So, I pulled my hand from my pocket and reached for the zipper on the side of my briefcase, headed for my wallet. And the voice said, "We both know that's not what I'm talking about."

And that's when I kicked the trash can next to me, scratched at an imaginary itch on my neck, and, seeing no acceptable way out, asked the fellow if he wanted a cup of coffee. He nodded tentatively. I motioned to the Market Coffee Shop about a half block up the street and we walked in silence to the door and went in.

I said, "I'm Sam," and held out my hand. He didn't take it. Instead he held his hands up so I could see the dirt crusting his palms. We stood inside the door for a minute while this wreck of a human being tried in vain to tell me his name. Finally, I was made to understand that his name was Jim, or that calling him Jim was close enough.

I suggested that Jim wash up while I got us something to drink and something to eat. "What would you like?" I said. Jim stammered out ba-ba-ba-lack... and then gave up—shaking his head slowly in a dejected sort of way. So, I went off saying not to worry, that I'd get us something good. And he wandered back to the bathroom.

It took a while but I finally got two big black coffees, a couple of pre-packaged ham sandwiches and some huge chocolate chip cookies. I put all of this down on a table and stood looking around for Jim.

I waited a long time. I began to think he had left, but then Jim appeared by the table and held out his hands for my approval. I said they looked great to me and suggested that we sit down and dig in, but he didn't move. He held out his hand. I took it, and we were properly introduced.

After he sat down, he looked at me—not at the air beside my head. He still looked at the world through that awful matted hair of his. And then he bowed his head and folded his hands in front of him and offered a silent prayer.

I'm quite sure I appeared completely dumbstruck to Jim. If I did, it's because I was. How could this shell of a human possibly be offering thanks for anything?

After that, the awkwardness and discomfort between us seemed to melt away.

Jim was obviously starving. His hands shook so violently when he tried to open the sandwich wrapper that I took the sandwich from him and unwrapped it while he waited… patiently.

He ate deliberately and occasionally looked over at me but didn't try again to speak. I watched him and dodged the uncomfortable stares of the folks seated around us. I told Jim about coming over to Seattle from Walla Walla on business for a few days and how nice it was to be back downtown for a while. I rattled on about living on a farm and learning about weeds and coyotes and how a stream could meander and wash away your pastures. Jim nodded and seemed to be interested, but didn't try to speak.

When he'd finished his sandwich, the cookie, the half of my sandwich I didn't eat, my cookie and an entire cup of coffee, I asked if he wanted anything else. He shook his head, got up, gathered up the remnants of our lunch and headed for the trash can. I followed him to the door. I think he was trying to dodge those uncomfortable stares, too.

We stepped back out onto the street where pedestrians parted to avoid us. I handed Jim $5 and offered my hand again.

Jim looked at my hand and started searching his pockets—trying each in turn—then starting over again until he found what he was looking for. He pulled a key from his pocket, looked at me carefully and directly, took my hand, placed the key in my palm and closed my fingers around it. I asked him what it was for and for the first time Jim sort of smiled. He turned and walked away.

The key now rests in a bowl on a table next to my desk that's full of paperclips and other stuff.

Wiese's Mayonnaise

Now, I know you are wondering why a guy like me would include a mayonnaise recipe in this book. What could be so special about mayonnaise, anyway?

Well, I'm here to tell you that this mayonnaise is something very special. It is way better than anything you can buy in the store and makes a treat out of left-over turkey on white bread with tomato and lettuce.

This recipe includes a raw egg. I have eaten Wiese's mayonnaise all my life and am still here to tell about it, but if you're worried about getting sick, just go out and get some store-bought mayonnaise.

Wiese's Mayonnaise
Makes 2 cups

Ingredients
2 cups vegetable oil
1 egg
2 tablespoons lemon juice
1/4 teaspoon dry mustard
1 teaspoon salt
1 teaspoon sugar
1/8 teaspoon paprika

Put all of the ingredients except the oil in a food processor and blend until well combined. With the food processor running, add the oil in a fine stream *very slowly* until you achieve the consistency you want. Refrigerate Wiese's Mayonnaise for up to a week.

The next two recipes will benefit from using Wiese's Mayonnaise.

A False God

Dear Deb:

You asked how my writing career is going; I'm guessing that by the end of this report you'll wish you hadn't. My new profession is giving me an up close and personal view into your publishing world. Some of your early advice is beginning to sink in.

Sorry I'm such a slow learner.

You will be pleased to know that I have started studying on the craft of writing. Yes, you're right; maybe I should have studied writing before I started writing, but better late than never, I guess.

A little over a year ago—when my first book came out—the occasional person would read it and catch me on the street and suggest I go get a book by Anne Lamott entitled *Bird by Bird*—that I'd probably enjoy reading it. Well, I'd heard of Ms. Lamott but hadn't read any of her books.

I assumed that my readers were saying that my engaging style of writing is similar to hers and that I'd get a kick out of reading something so rich and entertaining. I certainly did not know that she is both a writer and a writing instructor and that her book is entertaining reading on the subject of writing.

In retrospect, I guess those kind souls were looking for a nice way to nudge me into writing therapy. So okay, I've gotten the message and I'm now trying to get the horse back in front of the cart—so to speak.

Since I've read Ms. Lamott's book, I've discovered a bunch of other writing books and online help. I have read up on "genres." I've found that the word "genre" is a bookish sort of word—the kind of word that a writer can throw around to demonstrate his writer-hood—and therefore worth knowing.

I have also read up on style and character development and grammar. I've completed writing exercise after writing exercise. I'm even thinking about springing a few bucks free from my wallet and going off to a writing conference where the talent of others will have an opportunity to rub off on me.

In other words, I want you to know that I'm taking your advice seriously… I just don't know how much is sinking in.

When I sit down to write, I start off with good intentions and a willingness to experiment. I look for opportunities to stretch myself—at least for a little while. And then I lapse back into ways that are comfortable for me and just start typing up the words that stumble out of my brain pretty much in the order my brain suggests. It's easier.

Now I'm guessing that you'll say something like, "But Sam, if you'd keep on struggling with new ways of saying things, your writing would improve and your audience would grow and you'd become a famous author and get on Oprah."

Okay, I hear you, but I'm finding that I like my little

group of good and loyal readers and they seem to like my writing just the way it is. More and more, I'm thinking I'll just stick with them.

Oh, I'll experiment from time to time and I think a writer's seminar would be interesting, but I'm guessing that doing what's comfortable is the way to go.

I'd be more concerned about it if I thought that the great American novel was in here somewhere trying to find its way out of me but I don't think I'm running any real risk of denying my country its defining tome. I keep remembering the one creative writing course that I took in college and my professor asking me every so often if I had any interest in a business career or maybe flipping pancakes for a living.

Now, I hate to tell you this because I'm afraid you'll just give up on me: I'm finding that the publishing part of being an author is a bit of a drag on my daily contentment index.

I'm not talking about the money part; I never really expected writing to fill up the McLeod family coffers—particularly when you factor in the rate at which we McLeods can shed ourselves of dollar bills. I've often thought that our money spending would be a lot more efficient if I just got the whole family into my truck and we drove through town throwing money out the window while yelling, "Come and get it while supplies last."

No, I'm talking about the time spent on getting books printed. I've done that now—three times. I've worked with some very nice Walla Wallans along the way and we've mostly had a good time. But, like I said, I've done that now. I'm way more partial to the writing part than I am to the publishing part.

Sometimes that starts me thinking that I should go find an agent who will find me a publisher who will take over all the publishing tasks. But Anne Lamott says "getting published" is not all it's cracked up to be—what with all the contract stuff, public acclaim, unbelievable riches, and so on. So, I'm just not into "getting published" anymore. It is a false god... I keep telling myself that. And I'm figuring that if I act like I don't want to get published, there's a better chance that I'll get lucky... and get published.

That brings me to the important subject of book promotion. This is a part of the process that I actually do like. It gets you out among folks who mostly enjoy what you're doing and want to say nice things to you. I am finding that I have an ego sufficiently large to soak up all the compliments anybody has to offer about my books. There aren't many admirers; I'll grant you that. But my few admirers are good people who know what they like and are willing to share their admiration with me. Annie is always saying about herself, "I like people who like me." Well, I like people who like my books.

I've now given a few book-related talks. I've even done a program at the Walla Walla Country Club, so my book writing is getting me into at least one place that wouldn't otherwise have me. I'm getting ready to do book readings and signings at several other stops around town and in places like Pullman, Spokane, and even Seattle. The gatherings aren't what you'd call standing-room-only where readers climb over one another, desperate for my autograph, but the few folks who show up are engaging and we have plenty of time to chat. We make up in quality chat time what my signings lack in number of participants.

A few weeks ago, I went to do a couple of book signings up in Pullman where Washington State University is located. In the afternoon, I mostly sat at a table in the local Barnes & Noble, played with my pens and my new book signing ink stamp, and thumbed through the gluten-free diet books that were within reach of my chair.

Then I got interested in watching folks wander in, notice that I was an author doing a book signing, and realize that if they came my way (which was the most direct route into the store) they'd probably have to talk to me, hear about my books, and then get their arms twisted so hard they'd buy a book they didn't want. It was really entertaining to see how far out of the way they'd go to avoid that horrible fate.

I didn't sell even one book until Jon and Mary, friends from Walla Walla, happened to walk in. They were in Pullman to visit an old professor of Jon's and had arrived a little early. So they wandered into Barnes & Noble to kill time. It was quite a coincidence.

Well, that gave us an opportunity to chat and catch up. It also gave me an opportunity to quiz them about all the folks they were buying Christmas gifts for and tell them how clever they'd be to give everybody on their list my books. In a matter of minutes I'd sold fifteen books and caused good friends to wish they'd stayed in Walla Walla.

Just before Christmas, I did a book signing at The Book & Game Company here in Walla Walla that was

pretty well attended. Jeffrey, who's done the artwork for my books, was there with me. That may account for the big turn out. The fact that Janice was out on the side-walk in front of the store sweet-talking passers-by may also have helped. It's hard to tell. So, for the first time there was a little bit of a line to get books signed.

I noticed an old codger hanging out on the periph-ery of the crowd. He had his Dekalb Seed hat in his hand and badly matted hat hair to prove that he'd been wearing it. He wore his coverall pant legs stuffed into the tops of his rubber work boots. He'd show up and watch what we were doing for a minute or two and then disappear for a while. And then there he'd be again—hovering just out of speaking range. He looked curious but not particularly friendly.

Well, after an hour or so, the line dried up. Jeffrey and I were left to enjoy each other's company. And then there he was again—the old codger. He stood there in front of us for a few minutes and fingered a book that was lying on the table while we watched. Not a word was spoken. That is, until the old guy up and asked, "Which one of you boys wrote this book?"

It is a rare day that somebody refers to me as a boy, but compared to him I was.

"I did," I said.

"Is this book about Walla Walla?" he asked.

"Well, not really," Jeffrey explained. "It's more about a couple who moves from the big city to try their hand at country living."

The old man let this sink in. "Well, I've lived around here all my life; and my dad before me and my grand-dad before all of us. I don't reckon you boys have any-thing to teach me about Walla Walla."

And then he wandered off.

Now that I have written a couple of books and writ-ten stories about some of the characters who live in this valley—and there are plenty of them—I'm finding that the folks I meet fall into one of three categories: The Truly Uninterested, The Bean Spillers, and The Exceptionally Wary.

The Truly Uninterested could not care much less about me or my books. We tend to meet and part com-pany without a lot of wasted effort.

The Bean Spillers are dying to get in a book. A Bean Spiller would have the world understand what he already knows about himself—he is a uniquely inter-esting human being who should be best pals with Leno and Letterman but hasn't found a way to get his story out. These people will tell you everything about themselves. A Bean Spiller will show you the birthmark on his pubic bone if that'll get him into a book in a flattering way. Bean Spillers think they have nothing to hide, but most of them do... and they would do themselves a favor to figure that out.

And then there are The Exceptionally Wary—the folks that I'd like to get to know and who were actually becoming my friends until I put out that first book and exposed the fact that I sometimes write down what I see and hear... where other folks can get at it. The Exceptionally Wary sit across the breakfast table from me pushing their scrambled eggs around on the plate wondering how it is that I'll analyze them and misrepresent what they say. Taking notes only makes the whole situation worse.

So, the bottom line is that my writing initially made it easier to meet folks around Walla Walla but now acts as an invisible shield that keeps some folks at what they consider a comfortable distance.

One other thing: Authoring exposes the very worst my memory has to offer. I've never had a good memory. I don't think it's the result of dementia or some other age-related disease—unless of course these diseases can kick in as early as age 15. In my previous work lives, I've suffered, but somehow gotten by, with a pitiful power of recall. I tend to load facts just long enough to use them maybe once before pulling the plug and letting them get sucked into a file somewhere at the bottom of my brain called "permanently irretrievable items."

Unfortunately, good authoring requires something of a memory. Maybe that's one of the reasons I'm not hitting the *New York Times* Bestsellers List. I can generally compensate by collecting facts in small bites but it can get a little embarrassing when for the fourth time in ten minutes, I abandon the person I'm interviewing to make a quick run to the bathroom to scribble down notes in one of the toilet stalls. I can see my interviewee wondering why I don't just wear adult diapers. I know he'll never become more than an acquaintance because he'll be worrying about having to invite me over for dinner and thinking I might dribble on the carpet.

And how many times do you think I can forget the name of one of my good and loyal readers? "For heaven's sake," one will say. "I've introduced myself six times now and you still have no idea who I am." And the worst part is that she's right. Her face may look vaguely familiar, but I always get the context wrong. Somebody I've seen every day for the last two months at the bookstore may get filed by my brain into the middle of some hazy recollection about an acquaintance I made in Chicago back in 1979.

And her name? Well, just forget that. There's no way that's coming anywhere near the boundary of my consciousness.

So why won't I just admit it? Why won't I just say, "Geez, I'm sorry. I have a terrible memory for names and most everything else. Would you tell me your name again?" What's the worst that can happen?

But oh no, subconsciously I must be terribly embarrassed about my bad memory because I almost always try to bluff my way through it. I'll call somebody "hey, friend," or "chief" while hoping beyond hope that the name will come to me but knowing that it never will.

Thankfully, Annie's got all this down; she knows these little cues and will step up and introduce herself. Whereupon the person we've run into will say his name and save me from certain embarrassment. And then, of course, I'll say something like, "Oh, I'm sorry. I didn't realize you and Annie hadn't met. I should have introduced you"—pretending that I had remembered the guy's name all along.

Unfortunately Annie's not always there to save me, so after saying "Hi, Chief," I start stammering about the weather while my brain searches for the file that's permanently irretrievable, and it soon turns into a dead giveaway that I haven't the foggiest notion whom I'm addressing.

Last but not least, Deb, I have to tell you that there is something very appealing to me about sitting in my little writer's office here in downtown Walla Walla with books and papers piled up all around me. The view out onto the street is nice, and I have a fire engine red, velour-like nap sofa behind my desk that's there just in case the effort of writing wears me down— which it seems to do about 2pm every day right after lunch at T. Maccarone's. It's a nice retreat from the dizzying pace of life out here on the prairie.

Well, enough about my new career. I just wanted you to know that I'm doing the best I can between rejuvenating naps. Here's hoping that you and Don will get over here pretty soon.

Best,
SAM

Mother Mary's Potato Salad

My mother, Coco, makes some very good potato salad. Down below, I opine that Mary's potato salad is the best I've ever eaten. This is risky business because it is very likely that my mother will be the only person who ever reads this book. I'd hate to lose the one loyal reader I can count on. So, I'm engaged in something of a balancing act. You will notice that I've included three of my mother's recipes in this book. So I'm safe... I think.

* * * * *

I have only made this potato salad once. I felt like I had to do it once myself if I were going to include the recipe in this book. If you try it, I can promise you that you'll make it over and over again.

The reason I don't prepare it myself is this: I know Mary.

Whenever I start to think about potato salad, I stop by to see Mary. She's usually in her garden—a beautiful retreat right in the middle of town.

Now, I can't be too obvious about my real reason for stopping by, so I act like I'm checking in on Floyd, her husband. And in the course of conversation, I wiggle in something short but sweet about her potato salad—something like: "Hey, Mary, it's springtime in Walla Walla and the tulips are blooming and my how beautiful your garden looks and that reminds me of your potato salad because, other than your gorgeous garden, your potato salad is one of my favorite things about Walla Walla." And then she blushes and waves her hands and says, "Go on now... it's not all THAT good."

And then I say, "But Mary, it is! It's the best potato salad I've ever eaten."

Then Floyd will start nodding his head because he can see where I'm going with this. And he'll chime in, "He's right, Mary. Your potato salad is REAL good."

And then Mary will say, "Go on now... you two... I don't know what you're thinking... it's not THAT good."

And we'll put on our most sincere faces and say in unison, "But Mary, it is THAT good."

And then a couple of days later, Mary will call me up on the phone and say that she's made some potato salad—a bowl for them and a bowl for Annie and me—and that I should stop by next time I'm in town and pick it up. And I'll say, "Why Mary, you shouldn't have..."

And then I'll stop by the next day and Floyd and I will grin at each other while Mary fetches that big bowl of potato salad from the refrigerator.

We're good—Floyd and me. We're a good team. We know how to get us some good potato salad.

* * * * *

By the way, you might want to try making this potato salad with Wiese's Mayonnaise.

Mother Mary's Potato Salad
Serves 8 to 10

Ingredients

6 medium, unpeeled baking potatoes
1/2 cup minced onion
2 tablespoons white vinegar
1½ teaspoons salt
1/4 teaspoon freshly ground black pepper

1 cup minced celery
1/4 cup minced pimentos
1/4 cup minced dill pickle
4 boiled eggs chopped coarsely
1 cup mayonnaise
1 tablespoon Dijon mustard

Garnish: paprika, diced pimentos, chopped flat-leaf parsley, and/or quartered boiled eggs

Boil potatoes in their skins until cooked through but still firm. Cool potatoes slightly, peel, dice, and put into a large bowl. Add onions, vinegar, salt and pepper and toss just until combined. Refrigerate for one hour.

Add celery, pimentos, pickle, eggs, mayonnaise and mustard. Stir to combine. Garnish with paprika, diced pimentos, chopped flat-leaf parsley, and/or quartered boiled eggs if you like.

Refrigerate covered until cold. It's even better if you can refrigerate it overnight.

This potato salad is good with most anything... or even by itself. I've been known to eat a small bowl of Mary's potato salad for breakfast.

Rotary

Here's another Larry. I am blessed with an abundance of friends named Larry...

Dear Larry:

Well, I joined Rotary. My YMCA buddies, Lou and Les and Russ, finally got through to me that Rotary would be a great way to meet people and get involved in the community. And yes, I do remember that you told me the same thing several months ago.

Last week, I got a call from Lawson who's in charge of lining up speakers for the Rotary lunch we have every week over at the Marcus Whitman Hotel. He started off the conversation congratulating me on the good sense I'd shown by joining Rotary. I thanked him and said I was glad to be aboard—genuinely impressed that a fellow Rotarian would go out of his way to call me up and make me feel a part of things.

But as I began to think that our telephone call was coming to a close and started saying my goodbyes, he said, "Hang on there, Sam. I've got a question to ask you."

"Sure, what's that?" I replied.

"How about you come to the Rotary meeting next

week and make a speech to us?"

"Oh, Lawson... Geez, that's very kind of you to ask... but I don't do public speaking."

"Now come on, Sam," he says. "You're being too modest."

"Oh, no I'm not," I say. "I'm being honest. I'm barely an author. I just started writing books a few months ago. I'm not sure I'm very good at writing, but I'm quite sure I'm no good at public speaking..."

"Well, Sam," he interrupts. "I'm responsible for finding our lunch speakers—every week for a full year."

"Wow, that's a big job," I say.

"Yes, it is," says Lawson. "It's tough to find something new and different for our lunch talks and that's why I'm calling you, Sam."

And I said, "Well, that's really nice, like I said, but you don't want me. I don't do public speaking."

"Now, now, Sam," he says. "You're not letting me finish what I'm trying to tell you. I've gotten us a speaker every week thus far this year—that's 46 speakers—and I'm sitting here looking at my calendar and I don't have anybody lined up for next Thursday yet; and I've called everybody I can think of; and I can't find anybody interesting to come talk to us next week; and that's why I'm calling you."

"Oh, I see," I say. "So you don't care if I can speak. You're a desperate Rotarian just trying to do his job. And you don't want to fail. You just need as warm body to stand at the podium next Thursday and talk for 30 minutes. You've run out of interesting folks to buttonhole, so you're down to me. Have I got that

Rotary

right?" I say.

"Well, Sam," he says. "That might be a little strong—the way you said it, I mean. But, basically you're right. So, come on Sam. You can do it. You can talk on anything you'd like—just agree to speak. I'll put a nice note in your Rotary file if you do."

Now, I have done a lot of stuff in my life. That means that there are plenty of files in my past. And near as I can guess, there aren't a lot of nice notes in my files. So, all of a sudden, Lawson had hit on one of my lifelong regrets—too few nice "notes to file." My "notes to file" could stand a little beefing up with nice notes. So, that's when weakness overtook me and I agreed to do it. But I'm really not a public speaker.

So what was I going to do? What would I make a speech on? I didn't have a lot of time—just a week.

It normally takes me much longer than that to think up something interesting to say. I had to scramble. So, I figured I'd go take a peek into the big blue Rotary folder I'd been given when I became a Rotarian. Maybe I could find a subject in there and maybe that would lead to some interesting thoughts.

And I found one. And it ended up turning into a speech that I could give. And here's the speech I gave:

Rotary Speech—November '05

Helpful hint: Envision one very nervous guy trying to mumble out words through a thick Southern drawl while looking at a room full of folks with their arms folded over full bellies—some actively nodding off.

Good afternoon, fellow Rotarians. Lawson called

me last week and buttonholed me into speaking today. He said he couldn't find anybody interesting to talk to you today. So, here I am.

Now, before I launch into the very important and timely things I have to say, I need to tell you that I don't do public speaking. Yes, I have written a couple of books, which you all should have bought by now in an effort to be supportive of a fellow brother in Rotary. But the fact that I can write words down on paper does not mean that I can speak. I don't know if I can do public speaking. So, we're all embarked here on a little experiment for the next 30 minutes—which is how long Lawson says I have to talk before he'll write a nice note to my Rotary file. If you're feeling a little like a guinea pig, I'd say your instincts are holding up pretty well.

The last time I was up here at this podium was the day I became a member of Rotary. Les introduced me and Linda gave me a big blue folder full of more information about Rotary than any right-thinking human being could possibly want to read. Linda also gave me my Rotary badge—a bright, shiny red badge with my name on it. After I'd been introduced, I walked back to my table through some polite applause to where John and Earl and Les and Bill and Steve and Margaret were sitting. They all congratulated me on my acceptance into the Club.

And that's the first time I noticed it; everybody sitting at the table had a *blue* Rotary badge. And I'd just been given a *red* Rotary badge. I was confused. Why did all my Rotary brothers and sisters have blue badges? And why had I gotten a red badge? Like I said,

I was confused. I wanted to belong; I thought I'd made it; but the red badge/blue badge thing was suggesting to me that I hadn't. I was still somehow different.

It didn't seem appropriate to start whining about getting a different colored badge right after I'd become a member. So instead of quizzing my tablemates, I resolved to take my confusion home with that big blue folder and see whether there was an answer in there somewhere before I started complaining about being singled out for special treatment.

Well, I got home that night and lugged that folder into my office and plopped it down on my desk. I almost sat down to find the answer to the blue badge/red badge thing, but thought better of it, and went and opened a bottle of wine and poured Annie and me a glass and joined her out on the porch where she sat knitting a sweater. And then I made a new resolution to get up early the next morning and dig in on my badge question when I was fresh.

The next morning I got up early. I took a shower and brushed my teeth; and I put on my farmer jeans and an old fleece pullover and sat barefoot at my desk. I opened the blue folder and faced a mountain of paper—some pages with pictures on them, but mostly pages full of fine print. I figured the answer to my badge question was probably buried there somewhere in the fine print. I hate to admit it, but I started to feel a little like I should have asked for the folder full of fine print *before* I'd joined up.

Anyway, there on top was a page entitled "The Four-Way Test." The print was big and easy to read, so I started there and read on. The first "test" was this: *Is it the TRUTH?*

"Is what the truth?" I said to myself. I was staring at a pronoun that had no antecedent—no way to identify what "it" was. And then I read on and came to understand that as a Rotarian, I was expected to speak, think and do the "truth" in everything I spoke, thought and did.

And it struck me that I had just found a very good reason for not being a Rotarian. I began to feel that the Rotary thing was all a big mistake because... I don't *do* the truth.

No, no, I do not *do* the truth. I am a writer. I take things I observe or think up and I stretch them a bit. I fluff them up. I "embellish" them. Okay, I "exaggerate" sometimes. I don't exactly *do* the truth.

Now, it will not surprise you to hear that what I call "exaggeration," Annie calls "lying." And when I called out into the kitchen from my little office to tell her what I'd found as the first test of being a compliant and good Rotarian, she came in to look over my shoulder at the Four-Way Test, and shook her head.

Then she said, "No way. There's no way you can be a Rotarian. You don't qualify. You are an inveterate, unrepentant, incorrigible liar. You have been ever since I've known you. And your lying has gotten a lot worse since you started writing books."

Annie climbed up on her soapbox and started wagging her finger at me and speaking with such emotion that she was spitting. She concluded her little speech by saying, "And if you're not careful, Sam, some day your lying is going to cause trouble to come crashing down on you from Heaven above and it'll heap up around you so deep that you won't be able to see or even breathe."

You may be able to tell from this little speech and the finger wagging that Annie grew up in the South... and went to church a little too often...

But she had a point and I knew it. For a few seconds, I thought about listening to her.

It might be helpful for you to know that Annie and I have been married for over thirty years now. For the last thirty-plus years she has been uncovering personal flaws in me with frightening regularity. And finger wagging seems to be part of each and every flaw discovery. So, finger wagging is nothing new to me and I'll admit that I tend to ignore it more often than Annie would like.

She is still trying to figure what sort of pig-in-a-poke she got herself hooked up with on the day we got married, and is feeling a little bit hoodwinked by all of the shortcomings that she has discovered in me.

I don't want you thinking that I intentionally hid all my personal flaws from her before we were married—maybe a few, but certainly not all. No, no. It has taken thirty years of being married to a good woman for me to find out about all of my personal flaws. And unfortunately there's a very long list that Annie carries around in her head that she can spew forth whenever the occasion calls for it—and sometimes when the occasion does not call for it. My tendency toward exaggeration is right at the top of her list.

"So," I said to Annie. "What can I do? I want to be a Rotarian and I want to be a contributing member of the community. And I want to write books."

And she said (with great conviction), "You can't have it both ways this time, Sam. You're always trying to have it both ways and too often you get away with it. But not this time. This time you're stuck. You have to choose—writing and the path to trouble and misgiving *or* Rotary and the path to truth and clean living. What'll it be, Sam?"

Well, I said I'd have to think on it. And that night at dinner I confided to Annie that I had come to a decision. I'd chosen Rotary and the right path. And Annie let out a "Hallelujah." And one "Amen." And then she said that I'd made the right choice for a change, but that choosing was different from doing. And that the real question was, how I was going to learn to tell the truth?

I said I didn't know—that I hadn't thought that far ahead yet. And she said that I was in luck, because she had already thought it through and figured I'd need therapy—lots of therapy—regular weekly sessions with a psychoanalyst for several years to figure out where in my sordid past I'd gone off track and started down the path of falsehood and deception. And while I was at it, maybe she could make a list of all my other personal failings, and the therapist and I could work on those, too.

Well, I didn't have years to figure this out. I had chosen Rotary and truth telling, and had to get on with it. I didn't figure my Rotary brethren would be all that excited about granting me a truth-telling exemption while I underwent psychotherapy. No, I had to figure this thing out. Get to the root of my problem on my own. And get on with telling, thinking and doing the truth.

That night, I went to bed and read for a few minutes before drifting off. I fell into a very deep sleep and I began to dream. I was transported back in time to my first grade classroom—Mrs. Galloway's classroom—at HG Hills Elementary School just off of Davidson Road in Nashville, Tennessee. There I was—little Sammy McLeod—sitting in the back row of the line of left-handed desks, looking out the window where some older kids were playing on the playground. That is mostly what I did in first grade. I was not what you'd call a model pupil.

All of a sudden, I heard my name called. "Sammy McLeod," Mrs. Galloway was saying, "Come on up here for Show & Tell and share whatever it is you have for us today."

Uh-oh... I didn't have anything to share. I'd forgotten that it was my Show & Tell day. I got this sick feeling in my stomach and my bowels started to churn. I wasn't prepared. Next thing I knew, I was slowly walking to the front of the classroom where I stood next to Mrs. Galloway's desk and faced my classmates—all 22 of them. I looked at them for a very long time and mostly tried to suck down oxygen. And then I started to speak.

Without knowing where I was going with it, I started telling a story about how the entire McLeod family had driven out to the country on Sunday—just the day before—to a farm way out in the middle of a big cotton field, to a farmhouse surrounded by big trees up on top of a big hill looking out across the big cotton field... where a really nice man who was a friend of my dad's

167

was raising Labrador Retriever puppies. And how the friend had a new litter of 8-week-old puppies. And how my dad said that I was old enough to get a dog of my own and that my brothers and I should pick one out to take home.

I told about my new puppy named Bud who had big brown eyes, large floppy ears and huge paws, who just loved playing with a ball. And how my brothers and I had played ball all day with Bud in our backyard at home. And how after dinner that night, my mother and I had put down some newspaper in the guest bathroom on the tile floor where a little puppy mess would be easy to clean up. And how we had turned out the lights and left Bud in there all alone where he whimpered pitifully well into the night. And how, after everybody had gone to bed, I had snuck out of my room and down the hall and rescued Bud and brought him back into my bed with me where he curled up beside me with his cold little nose planted in my armpit. And how Bud and I slept all night just like that— just Bud and me.

Well, I mean to tell you that all my classmates were wide-eyed and their mouths were hanging open. They loved my story. And I loved telling it. Oh, how I loved telling it and seeing them hanging on my every word. And oh, how I loved the feeling that all of a sudden I was somebody. I was no longer little Sammy McLeod who most folks overlooked and didn't notice sitting in the last row of left-handed desks back by the window that looked out onto the playground. Nope, now I was Sammy McLeod the puppy owner and all of a sudden a very popular guy. And I really, really liked that.

There was, however, one small problem. The story was a complete fabrication—what Annie would call a big lie.

That afternoon, when school let out, I ran out of Mrs. Galloway's classroom and down the hall to the front door of the school surrounded by adoring class-mates who were dying to come by my house and see Bud. When I got to the street curb outside, I found Mrs. Groover's car and jumped in. It was Mrs. Groover's day to drive the hookup, and Tom and Linda and Jimmy were already in the car and they were whooping and hollering to Mrs. Groover that she should take me home first because that way we'd all be able to see Bud, Sammy's new puppy. And Mrs. Groover got a funny look on her face and said she hadn't heard about a new puppy and that's when I told her the story about going to get Bud just the day before and that was why she hadn't heard about it yet.

We drove down Jocelyn Hollow Road—one excited bunch of kids. I had started to believe the story myself, so it wasn't until we turned in to the McLeod family driveway that I settled on the problem I was facing. So, I piped up and said how sorry I was. I'd forgotten that my mom was taking Bud to the vet to get his puppy shots. He wouldn't be home when we got up to the house. We turned the corner around the side of the house and Mrs. Groover spied my mom's car and said how lucky we all were and how now we'd be able to see Bud.

I said no, no, no, I had forgotten to tell them that my mom was having some trouble with her car and was afraid to drive it, so she'd gotten Mrs. Cole, our next door neighbor, to take her and Bud to the veterinarian. I jumped out of the car saying that they'd all be able to see Bud the next morning when they came to pick me up. I ran to the back door and disappeared into the house before we could run into the need for additional fabrication.

Well, the next morning arrived and I was dreading school. Mrs. Sanders pulled up at our back door and I bolted out of the house and jumped into her car before my hookup mates could all pile out and start asking a bunch of tough questions about seeing Bud. I explained that my dad was taking Bud on a long walk up in the hills that surrounded the little valley where we lived before he went to work, so Bud wasn't there for everybody to see. I suggested that we should just drive on to school real quick and wait to see Bud after school that afternoon when Mrs. Sanders picked us up.

Mrs. Sanders pulled out of our driveway headed to school but started asking a bunch of probing questions about why my dad was taking an eight-week old puppy on a long walk up in the hills when she suspected that my dad had never set foot up in those hills—ever—before today...

I guess my answers weren't quite as crisp as I might have liked because, to make a very long dream mercifully short, that afternoon Miss Fuson from the principal's office came to Mrs. Galloway's room and interrupted class and whispered to Mrs. Galloway about something. Then Mrs. Galloway called out my name and asked me to come with her, and explained to the class that Miss Fuson was going to fill in for her while she and I went for a little walk down to Mrs.

Hearn's office. Mrs. Hearn was the principal. I did not take that as a good sign.

When Mrs. Galloway and I arrived at Mrs. Hearn's office, there were my mother, Mrs. Sanders, Mrs. Groover, my dad, and, of course, Mrs. Hearn—all gathered there to greet me. There were so many folks in Mrs. Hearn's office that Mrs. Galloway and my dad had to bring in a couple of chairs so everybody would have a seat. And then we all had a too-long conversation about Bud, and making up stories, and telling the truth, and how important that was, and how there'd likely be some consequences to deal with when I got home that afternoon. I was not having a very good day.

And that's when I woke up from my dream and lay there letting it all sink in. I came to understand how and when I'd gone off the truth-telling track. And why I liked making up stories. What I understood for the first time was this: I'm a not very interesting person without a little embellishment. The things I have to say are "less than interesting" without a little "improvement." But if I stretch things out a bit, fluff them up, and enhance the facts here and there, I can tell interesting stories and folks will like hearing what I have to say, and I'll be somebody—I'll be popular and adored.

Without embellishment, I'm nobody.

I got up and went on into town. I was dreading meeting folks on the street. I knew that I had to tell the truth—that I had to honor my Rotary oath—but I feared the worst. I feared that I'd bore folks to copious tears.

Well, I bumped into new Walla Walla friends all day long. I'd stop and talk to them, being very careful to be truthful in everything I thought, said and did—just like I'd promised myself and my brothers and sisters in Rotary. And I watched as folks started to fidget early on in conversations, fiddling with the keys in their pockets. They started saying how sorry they were that they'd forgotten that they needed to be somewhere else and needed to run, but, hey, how much they hoped we'd get together again real soon.

And there it was—proof in the pudding. I was now a truthful but boring person. My worst fears were being realized. I got depressed. I spiraled down. I drove home. I moped my way into the house where Annie greeted me with a slight grin on her face. It is not nice to find amusement in another human being's misery.

She asked me how it had gone—my first day of truth-telling—and I told her my sad story about being a truthful but boring person who'd had to give up the writing and storytelling he so dearly loved, to follow the path of righteousness. And how there was no point in trying to get to know more folks in our new town of Walla Walla because folks would figure out pretty quickly that I wasn't worth even a short howdy-do.

Annie sat staring at me. Finally, she whispered, "Sam, honey, haven't you figured this out yet? I know you can be a little slow on the uptake, but you should have gotten it by now."

I responded with a frown and a slow, dejected shake of my head.

"Sam, honey, don't you understand now why we were led to Walla Walla and our new lives here? And why you were led to Rotary where you could come to terms with your devilish and lying ways and get back

on the path to righteousness? And don't you understand why all those other Walla Wallans are members
of Rotary?

"Well no, I guess I don't," I said.

"Now, Sam, honey, think it through. What do you
know about all of your brothers and sisters in
Rotary?"

Instead of slowing down so I could respond, Annie
just went on ahead and answered her question: "All of
those Rotarians are truth-tellers. That means that,
underneath it all, they're 'less than interesting' people
just like you are. And that's why they're gathered
together in a club. It's really just a fancy support group
where 'less than interesting folks' go to be among folks
who are just as uninteresting as they themselves are."

And the light dawned and it all made sense to me.
Annie was right.

* * * * *

So, my brothers and sisters in Rotary, I stand up
here at the podium before you today with a glad heart.
I have come here today to say how honored and
relieved I am to be one among many "less than interesting," but truth-telling folks on the righteous path.

Now I get it. And I'm proud of the great service
Rotary of Walla Walla provides to the community—
it's a great place for "less than interesting" people to
gather together and be supportive of one another, and
a great blessing for the Walla Walla community at
large to have all of us off the streets where we can't
bring the whole town to the brink of depression with
our somniferous storytelling. And now that I think of

it, what a great service Rotary must provide to communities all over the world.

And that's when I came back in my mind to the original question: Why do I have a red badge when all the rest of my brothers and sisters in Rotary have blue badges? I found myself desperate to belong—to have a blue badge. I started lusting after a blue badge.

That worried me as I sat down in front of the big blue folder laid open on my desk. It occurred to me that an organization that required truth-telling might also prohibit things like "lusting"—which I still do from time to time—not as often as I used to but often enough not to want to give it up, too.

I read that blue Rotary folder. I read it cover to cover. I am relieved to report that Rotary does not prohibit lusting. It's okay to lust after a blue badge.

So that's where I'm headed now—to find out what I have to do to get a blue badge so I can truly belong. And I'm hoping that Lawson is going to go back to his office where he'll sit down and pen a nice note to my Rotary file...

Polite applause...

* * * * *

So, Larry, that was it, my first-ever speech. Folks tell me it went okay. I'm grateful for small blessings. And I'm glad it's over.

I'll be happy to get back to writing.

Best,
SAM

Coco's Cranberry Salad

This is a congealed salad my mother makes. It's good... real good. She made this every Thanksgiving and Christmas when we boys were growing up. After a while she learned to leave the chopped pecans and chopped celery out of the recipe, so we'd eat it. As you know, I cannot imagine why anyone would want to ruin good Jell-O salad with nuts or celery.

The word "salad" in the recipe name is a bit of a misnomer. But it has always played to my advantage, so I'm keeping it. Whenever my mother or an aunt or a grandmother would admonish us boys to eat our vegetables and salad, we'd turn straight to this Jell-O dish and dig in. This is my idea of salad.

So here it is. It was... and still is ... one of my favorites. Coco insisted I tell you that you can add a half-cup of chopped pecans and a half-cup of chopped celery to the recipe when you stir the cranberry sauce/sour cream mixture into the partially congealed Jell-O, but I'm not recommending it.

Coco's Cranberry Salad
Serves 6 to 8

Ingredients
1 small box raspberry Jell-O
3/4 cup boiling water
1 16-ounce can whole cranberry sauce
1 cup sour cream
Iceberg lettuce leaves and Wiese's mayonnaise for garnish

In a medium-sized bowl, dissolve the Jell-O in the boiling water. Put the bowl in the refrigerator for about 15 minutes until the Jell-O begins to congeal.

In a separate bowl, combine the cranberry sauce and sour cream. Stir the cranberry sauce/sour cream mixture into the slightly congealed Jell-O and pour into your favorite mold. Refrigerate until completely congealed.

Serve on lettuce leaves and add a dollop of Wiese's Mayonnaise on top if you like.

Grooted

In memory of a great teacher...

"Mr. Groot," I said. "I'm having a little problem with so-and-so who's not doing his job."
I explained the problem.

Mr. Groot sat there behind his desk and looked at me—no nods, no blinks, no changes in facial expression.

I said, "I guess I could do this, or that, or this other thing to encourage him to get back on track."

Mr. Groot sat there behind his desk and looked at me—no nods, no blinks, no changes in facial expression.

I said, "I think I'll try doing this first and see how it goes."

Mr. Groot sat there behind his desk and looked at me—no nods, no blinks, no changes in facial expression.

I said, "Thanks for your help, Mr. Groot."
At this, he nodded.

Walla Walla Sweet Onion Hush Puppies

This is a marriage made in Heaven—a southern staple wedded to a Walla Walla original.

You'd better make a bunch of these. Folks eat way more than they'll admit to.

The basic recipe calls for regular onions but I substitute Walla Walla Sweet Onions. I include Walla Walla Sweet Onions in recipes where I can, to support the neighbors and encourage their continuing generosity. Brilliant culinary instincts, don't you think?

Feel free to experiment. Try adding a tablespoon of minced jalapeno peppers along with the onions.

Walla Walla Sweet Onion Hush Puppies
Makes 20-25 puppies

Ingredients
Peanut oil for deep frying
1/2 cup all-purpose flour
1 cup stone-ground yellow corn meal
1½ teaspoons baking soda
1/2 teaspoon salt
1/4 cup minced Walla Walla Sweet Onion
1 cup buttermilk
1 egg, beaten

Pour the oil 2 inches deep in a heavy pot and heat to 365°.

In a large bowl, mix together the cornmeal, flour, baking soda and salt.

In a separate bowl, mix together the buttermilk and egg.

Pour the buttermilk/egg mixture into the dry ingredients, add the Walla Walla Sweet Onion, and stir just until combined.

Drop batter in small spoonfuls into the oil and fry the hush puppies until browned all over—just 1 to 2 minutes.

Remove the hush puppies from the oil and drain on paper towels.

Serve hot with butter...

Wedding Dad

Well, it's happened. Summer and her boyfriend, Rusty, have announced their engagement and have set a wedding date in June. It's big news around the McLeod household. Annie and I couldn't be happier.

The wedding plans have been in the making for almost five months now. It turns out that five months is not really enough time for proper wedding planning; so Summer, her mother, and Rusty's mother have been hard at it. We're almost there.

In the course of all the wedding doings, I have learned that fathers don't have much to do with weddings. "Get the wine," they said. "Make sure the wine gets there on time," they said. That was my only real wedding job.

"Show up, smile a lot and be pleasant," they said. It sounded more like a warning than a request for assistance.

"By the way," they said, "bring your wallet... the big one."

Unfortunately for you good and loyal readers, the lack of wedding duties has left me free to muse on the past. This wedding is stirring the memory pot—making me long for days I can't get back.

Memories are a bittersweet thing. But that's a lot of what I have now. So thank goodness for the memories.

* * * * *

When Summer was three years old, Jolie was one year old and Marshall was a future event. As a young lawyer, I was working way harder than I had imagined possible—but not as hard as Annie was working. Her life was overflowing with motherly duties.

So, when I arrived home on summer evenings, Annie, Jolie and Summer would greet me at the door and, without fail, Summer would start her chant: "Dad, let's go swing... Dad, let's go swing... Dad, let's go swing..."

And I'd say, "Okay, okay, okay... Just let me change my clothes and we'll go swing." Summer just loved to swing.

We lived in a little box of a house with a postage stamp-sized yard out back. There was a sturdy old swing set out there—a solid steel structure from which heavy chains hung bolted into weathered wooden seats. The old thing had seen better days but still functioned as a swing set. An aggressive swinger could pump her way to the second story of our little house if she wanted.

Our yard was in full bloom. So was the neighbors' yard. Dandelions were everywhere. On our way to the swing set, hand-in-hand, Summer would kick dandelion seed balls until the air around us filled up with the cottony seeds. Summer was very good about picking a bouquet of the short-stemmed yellow flowers for her mother.

Our neighbors, Fred and Myrtle Stevens, had a big yard compared to ours. So their crop of dandelions dwarfed our own. Mr. and Mrs. Stevens were well up in their 80s. They moved slowly, but they moved. Every night after supper, the two of them would emerge from their rat-trap of a Victorian house, don their sunhats, put on their gardening gloves, and push a wheelbarrow full of dandelion fighting equipment out into the midst of the enemy.

Mr. Stevens would then identify their first victim. He'd point out the offending plant to Mrs. Stevens who would nod her acknowledgment. Next, Mr. Stevens would take up his weapon—a forked instrument designed specifically for the uprooting of dandelions—bend very slowly from his waist, reach out in slow motion, detach the dandelion from the earth, straighten himself up, and drop the mortally wounded plant into the wheelbarrow that Mrs. Stevens had wheeled up beside him.

The process was repeated very slowly over and over again, but with admirable persistence. While I pushed Summer on her swing, we'd watch the Stevens in their quest to eradicate dandelions—a war they were fighting, but not expecting to win.

I loved that time Summer and I had together most every summer night—just the two of us swinging on the swing set in the backyard.

One night as we watched the Stevens and chatted on about baby Jolie and how she had spit up on Annie's new party dress just as Annie was trying it on, Summer yelled out, "Stop, Dad... stop the swing... pleeeeeze stop."

I assumed there was some major problem—an injury or urgent need to find a bathroom—so I grabbed the swing and brought the swinging to an abrupt halt.

"What in the world is wrong, Summer?" I said.

"Nothing's wrong," she said. "I have a question."

"Well, it must be a very important question for you to give up swinging," I said. "What is it?"

"Not so loud, Dad. The Stevens will hear," replied Summer in a whisper.

"Hear what?" I said.

"My question, Dad," Summer answered with obvious frustration.

Then here it came—the question.

"*Are the Stevens dead?*" Summer inquired.

"Well, of course not Summer," I responded, "You can see them both right over there working in their yard. They're not dead."

"Are you sure?" Summer asked.

"I'm quite sure," I answered back. "What makes you think such a thing?"

"Well, you know how when you step on a cricket?" Summer went on, "You know how when you step on a cricket, it's dead but it keeps on wiggling for a while?"

"Yes," I said. "Go on."

"Well," Summer said, "I thought maybe the Stevens were dead but still wiggling—just like crickets do."

I laughed so hard I couldn't catch my breath and Summer, who is very susceptible to contagious laughter, laughed until she couldn't breathe—even though she didn't really understand what we were laughing about. And the Stevens interrupted the Dandelion Wars just long enough to inquire as to the source of our laughter and that sent us into stomach-cramping laughter all over again.

I finally recovered long enough to tell the Stevens what Summer had said. Myrtle laughed until tears streamed from her eyes and that started Summer laughing all over again. For the next several months, the Stevens told that story to anybody who'd stop on the sidewalk long enough to hear it.

* * * * *

I remember father/daughter Saturday breakfasts with Summer—just the two of us—at Charles Gourmet when we lived in Bethesda, Maryland on the edge of Washington, D.C.—fresh-squeezed orange juice, black coffee for me, elephant ears and cinnamony bear claws.

And, I remember trips on the subway to the National Gallery of Art where Summer and I would stand hand-in-hand admiring Renoir's painting of the girl with the hoop—just the two of us. After our gander, we'd walk back down the museum's granite steps to find the popcorn man, where we'd get a bag of popcorn, sit on a park bench, and feed the pigeons.

I remember reading late into the night once when Summer was about 7 years old. All was very quiet. I thought everybody but me was asleep. I was reading *A Prayer for Owen Meany* by John Irving—the Christmas pageant story in the book—and, again, laughing so hard that I got the hiccups. Summer heard me from her bedroom, came scurrying down the hall, and leaned on the edge of the bed while I re-read the story to her. We both laughed until the bed shook—just the two of us. Annie slumbered away.

I remember driving to the hardware store on Saturday mornings. Summer was the only one who'd go with me on these almost weekly pilgrimages. We'd roll the car windows down and sing "Diamonds on the Soles of Her Shoes" at the tops of our voices—just the two of us.

And then when we moved to Seattle, I remember Saturday breakfasts with Summer at the Surrogate Hostess on Capitol Hill where we'd watch the freaky people with purple hair and multiple eyebrow piercings while we ate the best cinnamon buns ever made.

I remember so many good times with Summer. We did simple little things together—just the two of us—

and oh, the fun we had. I miss those times with her, and also the many times like them with Jolie and Marshall. It's a father's lament…Wedding Dads can get a little nostalgic.

* * * * *

To Summer… my delightful daughter… thanks for the memories… May there be many more to come… And from now until the end of your time on this Earth, may you and Rusty do simple things together, and laugh so hard you can't breathe, and create your own memories—just the two of you.

And may we all live to hear the two of you tell your stories to our grandchildren…

Much love,
DAD

Grandmother's Oatmeal Cookies (via Coco)

Okay, here they are. These are the oatmeal cookies that we boys would fight each other for whenever we went to Jackson, Tennessee for a visit. As far back as I can remember, these oatmeal cookies were in a big tin on Grandmother's kitchen table every time we visited her. There was fresh, cold, frothy milk in the refrigerator. Grandmother would pour us each a tall glass of milk while we boys wrestled the tin open.

Grandmother's Oatmeal Cookies
Makes three dozen cookies

Ingredients
1/2 cup butter
1 cup packed brown sugar
1 egg well beaten
5 tablespoons whole milk
1¾ cups rolled oats
1/2 cup seedless baking raisins
1/2 cup broken nutmeats
1½ cups flour
1/2 teaspoon salt
1/2 teaspoon baking soda
3/4 teaspoon cinnamon
1/2 teaspoon ground cloves
1/4 teaspoon freshly ground nutmeg

Preheat oven to 350°.

Mix the recipe ingredients in order, combining well as you mix. Before adding the raisins and nutmeats, it helps to mix them with some of the dry ingredients. This keeps them from sticking together and insures better distribution in the batter.

Grease a cookie sheet with butter. Drop batter in teaspoonfuls onto cookie sheet. Bake for 12 minutes.

Yummy!

Yoda

Y oda the Corgi is my dog. We are a pair and we both know it. We pretend that he is a family dog. But we know better.

Some of you may have heard the story. Annie and I were introduced to Yoda at a horseshow down in Oklahoma City a couple of years ago. Daughter Marshall was riding in events all weekend. Between events, Annie and I had a lot of downtime. I'd read and Annie would walk. She'd walk the barn aisles all day long—up and back, up and back—looking at all the horses and chatting with the owners. Annie has a lot of nervous energy that she needs to work off each day. I'm into conserving energy.

On one of her forays, Annie met Jan, a lady from Lubbock, Texas whose two daughters were there to show off their riding skills. Jan had brought a litter of five Corgi puppies to the show believing that she'd find good homes for them—four little girls and one little boy.

The little boy dog was named Yoda because, even at his very young age, he had huge ears that stuck up on top of his head like big tents that sheltered his eyes and his longer than normal nose. The rest of him was a short-legged oblong ball of brown and white hair.

While his sisters barked and yapped up a storm, biting at each other and bickering about most anything that came to mind, Yoda wandered his barn aisle, savoring the barn smells and greeting everybody who came by with a wagging stub of a tail and an overactive tongue. He didn't bark at all but seemed to smile a lot. He loved sitting in Annie's lap while she talked to Jan.

Annie was smitten. But she didn't breathe a word of her new romance to me.

Occasionally I'd look up from my book and spy Annie searching out Marshall between events. The two of them would whisper for a while and then go running off together. I knew something was up. I also knew that I'd hear about it in time—after they'd conspired for a while about whatever it was and coordinated their stories.

Sure enough, soon they were back with the story of Yoda all figured out. The words "so cute" seemed to follow every seventh or eighth word. "Come on, Dad. Just come see him. He's so cute," Marshall begged.

"Come on, honey. It won't hurt to look at him. He's so cute," Annie said.

"We don't need another dog," I responded. "And I know how this works. You two must think I was born yesterday. First, it's 'just come look at him.' Then it's 'just hold him for a little while.' And then the owner, who's probably a very nice lady and very good at pointing out all of the puppy's good qualities while leaving out all the stuff about little messes on the carpet and chewed up bedspreads, launches in on your side. And the three of you gang up on me and plead like your lives depend on it for us to do a very dumb thing and get another dog. No way. I don't need to see cute little Yoda. We don't need another dog. End of story."

Well, he was cute... and he jumped right into my lap... and lay there nibbling on each of my fingers in turn while Annie and Jan settled on a price and figured out the logistics of getting Yoda into our hotel room where dogs were strictly forbidden, how to keep cute little Yoda quiet on his first night away from his mom, and how to fit him into a carry-on pet satchel and fly him home to Seattle.

Yoda started out in life as a big city housedog. Then we moved over here to Walla Walla and out onto the prairie. He is now a farm dog and, like everything else in his life, he finds the farm much to his liking.

He's a little older now. It takes him a few minutes to warm up his stubby legs in the morning. Once he's up and moving, he waddles like one of those spring-loaded toy dogs where the head moves forward while the tail tries to follow in an erratic pattern of fits and sudden starts. He limps occasionally—still suffering from the lasting effects of an old football injury—no joke, a football injury.

Once he achieves a full upright position and a bit of forward momentum, he cruises his domain, greeting Sam the Dog, Annie the Dog, BC the Barn Cat, Babe the Housedog and each of Annie's alpacas in turn. He makes the same little greeting tour every morning without fail. He then roams the fence line checking for pheasants, rabbits, turkeys and the occasional coyote

that may have gotten too comfortable around our place.

After his reconnaissance of the perimeter, Yoda makes his way to the back porch where the other dogs and BC are moaning for their breakfast. Of all our animals, only Yoda seems to understand that Annie will be out to feed them when she's good and ready. She will not be hurried. Whining only seems to delay things.

So, instead of whining, good old Yoda falls onto his side in the middle of the porch and rolls onto his back where he sprawls with legs splayed out exposing his privates to the world—a move we call "airing out." And there he waits patiently for his morning bowl of dog cereal.

Yoda's days seem to be filled with wonder and relaxation. Between frequent naps under the porch, he can be found romping around the yard with Big Frank, our newest baby alpaca; or inciting a riot among the other dogs; or chasing BC around the barn; or greeting the occasional visitor at the gate. Once I saw him lying flat on his back under the roofline after one of our intermittent rains trying to catch drops of water in his mouth. When one of the other animals is sick or upset about something, Yoda is there showing his concern. He will lie next to a distraught alpaca for as long as it takes for his charge to calm down.

In the evenings when Annie and I sit out on the porch, Yoda lies beside my chair—not begging for attention—just glad to be there with us. On nights that we don't venture out onto the porch, he sits at my study door looking in at us with big, moist eyes.

After dark, Yoda goes on patrol—leading the big dogs into mock battle with imagined, threatening intruders. Rarely, we do get a real intruder—a skunk or a muskrat or maybe an off-course owl who tries to roost under the porch eave. That's when our well-drilled guard dogs go into action and chase the var-mint off. These infrequent security breaches are cause for great excitement around the place and are wel-comed by the dogs as grand entertainment.

You are, by now, probably thinking that we are dot-ing parents who see no shortcomings in Yoda. Unfor-tunately he does have a few. He can be overly protective of a soup bone. He prefers to do his busi-ness in the herb garden where we'd prefer that he not. And he is unusually fond of finding a rotting animal carcass to roll around on—making sure that he coats himself thoroughly with the bad smell—generally a very bad smell.

So, okay, he still has a few little things to work on... but he's mostly a perfect dog... and he's a very good companion.

Annie's Orange Pecan Pie

Annie loves pecan pie. Actually, she loves most anything with sugar in it. Over the last few months, she's been working on pecan pie variations. The original recipe came from an ancient copy of *The Stuffed Cougar*, a cookbook from Annie's hometown of Richmond, Virginia. Of Annie's more recent variations, this is my favorite—pecan pie that doubles as dessert and an after-dinner drink.

Annie's Orange Pecan Pie
Serves 6

Ingredients
4 eggs, well beaten
1 cup brown sugar
½ cup dark corn syrup
½ cup light corn syrup
½ cup dark molasses
2 tablespoons melted butter
2 tablespoons Cointreau (or comparable orange liqueur)
1½ cups pecans
1/2 teaspoon vanilla
1 nine-inch piecrust

Preheat oven to 350°.

Beat eggs, syrup, molasses, butter, and Cointreau together until well combined. Fold in the pecans and the vanilla. Pour mixture into the piecrust and bake at 350° until firm—about 1 hour. Allow to cool on a rack for at least 30 minutes. Serve with a big scoop of vanilla ice cream.

This is a real crowd pleaser...

Weathering In-Laws

D ear Brett:

Sorry I haven't written sooner. The holidays snuck up on us faster than I expected and my "to do" list went into a tailspin. The girls were all home with boyfriends in tow and Annie's mom came for a visit. So, I skidded off track.

You might remember that Annie's family is some-what famous "back east" for the weather they carry around with them whenever they go on vacation. Annie's mom and older brother have well-documented histories of vacationing only in inclement weather. I hadn't experienced their special talent for a while, but the month of December brought it all back to me.

Annie and I were married over thirty years ago and went together for a couple of years before that. So, for about a third of a century now, I have had a front row seat at her family's events. Almost every year, we went with the rest of her clan to the beach—always in August and always at a Virginia or North Carolina beach in weather that was 95 degrees with 95% humidity. And almost every year Annie and I would join the family for a few days of sitting in the living

room of whatever cottage we were all staying in, looking out the big picture window through torrential
rains to a hazy view of the beach and the Atlantic
Ocean beyond.

These rainy days at the beach were so predictable
that Annie would get on the phone with her sister and
sisters-in-law weeks before a vacation to plan indoor
activities like trips to the nearest beach trinket shops
and local movie theaters where we could see "Jaws"
for the umpteenth time.

I started to think that it was just a beach-related
coincidence, but then we'd go to a country place outside of Richmond over New Year's and sit in the family room for several days looking out the big picture
window through torrential rains to a hazy view of a
huge tidal marsh and the Pamunkey River beyond.
There was not much shopping nearby—just the Pamunkey Indian Reservation gift shop that we visited on
the first rainy day each year. After that, we were con-
fined to the house where we played Charades for
hours on end, chased after the kids and their cousins,
and ate way too much food.

I could go on and on with stories of rain-soaked
vacations—including evacuations to escape hurri-
canes barreling down on us and hunkering down in
gale force winds and torrential rain to wait out tor-
nado warnings. But these stories would only reinforce
the vacation curse my in-laws suffer year after year.

After telling our vacation stories to anybody who
would listen, friends and business associates came to
believe in the curse. It got to the point where Aggie
and Sally and Mary and Tommy and Randy and

Bucky and, well, a bunch of other folks would start calling during the spring to find out where and when the in-laws were vacationing that year—so they could avoid that quadrant of the country for their own vacations.

Now, since we McLeods moved out to the west and our girls have grown up and moved off in different directions, we have found it difficult to get to east coast family events with regularity. My memory of the curse faded—at least until we moved over here near Walla Walla where we get only 10 inches of rain a year.

We moved into our new farmhouse early last January and enjoyed warm sunny days for the next three months—no rain or snow for three whole months. So you're probably saying to yourself, "How nice." But the only time there's any meaningful precipitation out here on the prairie is during the winter. We residents of the Walla Walla Valley depend on winter rains and snow to bank water for use during the dry summer and fall months.

So by early April, folks were getting nervous about the drought, and articles filled up the newspaper with dire warnings about water shortages, global warming, summer range fires and all manner of related natural disasters.

There wasn't much to joke about but I regularly told our Walla Walla friends not to fret too much—that Annie's mom was coming for a visit and would bring us some considerable rainfall. They'd laugh politely and try to move on while I'd say, "No, you don't understand; I'm being perfectly serious." They'd laugh politely again and try to move on.

Well, Annie's mom was scheduled to arrive on a Sunday in early April. On Saturday, a few clouds started to gather way up the valley at the edge of the mountains and folks started talking in hopeful whispers about the possibility of a little rain. By Saturday night, a solid bank of tall cumulus darkened the skies—no moon or stars visible for the first time in over 90 days.

On Sunday morning the clouds hanging over the farm started spitting occasional drops of rain—sort of like the sky was practicing but having trouble remembering how to rain. Grandma's plane left Seattle about 10am that morning scheduled to arrive in Walla Walla at 11am. By 10:30am, it was raining—hard.

On my way to the airport, I got a call from Ron asking when Annie's mom was coming in and I told him I was driving to the airport as we spoke. And he said, "I'll be damned. You really weren't kidding about the curse."

Grandma's plane landed in a torrential downpour and the Horizon Air greeters ran out in their rain gear to hand out umbrellas to deplaning passengers. We braved gale force winds and horizontal rain to load up in my rig and drove back out to the farm in a driving rain that blew tumbleweeds across the road in such numbers that they piled up and covered the fence lines along the highway.

Grandma stayed for five days and it rained pretty much full-time while she was here. Folks would stop us in town and ask to meet the lady that brought us some rain—mostly joking about the coincidence. But

Annie and I knew better.

On the morning of her departure, the sun poked through the clouds for the first time and Grandma got a brief look at our sunny little valley before she left, taking all the weather with her.

So, that was it. Near as I remember, it didn't rain again until November when we got a few tenths of an inch of rain—enough to register in the rain gauge out behind the barn if you ran out during the tail end of the rain to look before the hot dry air reclaimed the little bit of water in the bottom of the dish.

In the early fall, Annie's brother called from Virginia to say that he and his wife were coming out for Barrel Tasting Weekend where the local wineries show off their new wines. And I went back to folks around here and told them that Larry and Vickie were coming for a few days and that rain was on its way. As usual, they all laughed politely and tried to move on. And I'd say, "No, no, I really mean it. This is the kind of mystical stuff you can count on." And they'd laugh politely again and try to move on.

Sure enough, by the time the in-laws landed in Seattle to make the short connection into Walla Walla, the weather had deteriorated into serious freezing rain and occasional snow—something the surprised weatherman was calling "wintry mix." By the time they landed in Walla Walla, there were six inches of wintry mix on the ground. Steady rains for the next two days turned the snow to slush, and visiting wine sippers plodded through the muck. The day after Larry and Vickie left, our bright, sun-filled days returned and dried up all the rain—and the little spider went up the water spout again.

And then, just a week or so later, Grandma announced that she was accepting our invitation and was coming out for the Christmas holiday—ten full days of visiting. And I started telling everybody who'd listen not to lose heart—that more rain was on the way—ten full days of it. They'd laugh politely and try to move on. But I'd say, "No, I really mean it. Annie's mom is coming and she's somebody you can count on for rain. Don't you remember her last visit?" And again they'd laugh politely and try to move on.

Annie's mom arrived on the Thursday before Christmas, and like clockwork, the rain came down in buckets. That meant it was snowing big time up in the Blue Mountains; so our girls and their boyfriends donned their snow clothes and headed off for several days of great skiing up at Bluewood. The folks who run the ski resort were shocked at the snow piling up faster than they could groom it. And Grandma started to get calls from our Walla Walla friends—mostly folks she'd never met—thanking her for coming and asking whether she could come back again and stay for a couple of months—say mid-February through mid-April.

Well, Grandma who's always regarded the family's rainmaking skills as something of an embarrassment, started thinking that what passed for a curse on the east coast might actually be a blessing out here and maybe she could do some good with it. So, she's agreed to come back.

And now everybody around here is all excited. The City Council has passed a resolution authorizing the high school band to greet Grandma at the airport where Jerry, one of the Council members, will present Grandma with a key to the city. After she's settled in for a day or two and the rain has had a chance to fill up the rivers around here, Hal, one of the Public Works officials, wants to take Grandma on a tour of the Valley to see the fruits of her presence here.

Several of the local restaurants have already offered us free dinners during her stay and the Chamber of Commerce wants to hold a banquet in her honor in early March. And Merchants Delicatessen has offered to host a wine and cheese reception where Grandma will autograph "Walla Momma" T-shirts for anybody who wants to come by. (Just in case you've forgotten, "Walla" means water in the language of the Cayuse Indians who used to live in the Valley.)

Anyway, we're gearing up for a big time. It'll be interesting to see how her visit plays out. If the rains come like they're supposed to, the County has already hinted that they may want to talk with us about building Grandma her own place out here in the valley, stocking her refrigerator, and covering her expenses, including air fare, if she'll come out when needed. They admit that such an arrangement would be infinitely cheaper than most of the water conservation plans they're now considering.

Annie's brother, Larry, is beginning to wonder if there's money to be made by delivering rain to the valley, and is starting to negotiate with Grandma about a possible tag-team approach to the problem.

Well, I don't know what will come of all the talk. But it's nice to watch Annie's mom zip out the silver lining in that old black cloud that's been following the family around for so many years.

Stay in touch, Brett. We'd love to get you out to the farm... sometime when Annie's family is not visiting...

Best,
SAM

Wiese's Strawberry Pie

My aunt, Wiese, celebrated her 90th birthday back in January. She lived with us as a sort of second mom during my formative years. When my parents went off on a trip by themselves, Wiese took charge of the kitchen. And when Wiese took charge of the kitchen, we boys would start pestering her to make a few of her famous strawberry pies, so we'd have plenty of pie for dessert while the parents were out of disapproval range.

I must admit that I've never made this pie myself.

Wiese wrote up the recipe; she is an accomplished cook. Plus, Annie has tested the recipe several times now. Once again, you are in good hands.

Wiese's Strawberry Pie
Serves 8

Ingredients
8 cups strawberries
2/3 cup sugar
2/3 cup water
2 tablespoons cornstarch
1 baked pie shell (homemade, if you're up to it)

Cut the tops from the strawberries and cut in half. In a blender, blend 1 cup strawberries and the water until smooth.

In a pot, combine sugar, cornstarch, and contents of blender. Cook over medium heat and bring to a slow boil for a few minutes, stirring often until the mixture is well combined and nicely thickened.

Let the glaze cool. Then coat the pie shell with enough of the glaze to cover the bottom and sides.

Combine the remaining strawberries and glaze in a large bowl until strawberries are well coated. Then pour into pie shell and chill for a couple of hours in the refrigerator.

You can put a big spoonful of fresh whipped cream on top of your piece of pie, but why mess with a good thing?

A Secret Place

Annie and I have a very secret place out at the farm. It's a secret place down by the Walla Walla River hidden from view by the ash, cottonwood and willows that surround it. Annie tells everybody about it.

She is so pleased with herself. Annie discovered this little piece of solitude on one of her winter strolls down by the river when she and the dogs went off-path, through the loosely-stranded barbed wire fence, across a low place that can get pretty boggy during spring runoff, and through a jungle of prickly thistle. There it was—a small open grassy place surrounded by towering, leafless trees. Why it wasn't full up with thistle and willows is a pleasant mystery.

We have seen it through more than a year now—experiencing winter morning fog so dense that you can't see the next spot you're stepping on; spring drought that withered and browned new growth among the grasses and lent encouragement to our drought-loving weeds; a summer so hot and dry that even Walla Wallans were commenting on it; and a fall that brought the welcome relief of crisp, cool winds and much needed precipitation.

We've tried not to disturb it. Our peaceful glen sits very quietly there by the river filtering the river's roar into background sounds worthy of a New Age flute and sitar duet.

If you sit quietly in the grass, the edges of the glen come alive with nibbling rabbits, the incessant scratching and gnawing of our resident beaver, the songs of birds searching the brambles for the last of the unplucked berries, and the tentative yelps of coyote pups wondering where their mother has run off to.

Occasionally one of the pups will wander out of the den that couldn't be far from the clearing. He'll stick his nose out of the underbrush, sniff out your presence, make very brief eye contact, and then scamper back home.

The smells of the secret place vary from the sweet of honeysuckle to the roasted scent of sun-scorched cheat grass to the offensive aroma of a skunk nosing around nearby. Slowing down enough to recognize that my nose is smelling lots of smells, and then patiently focusing on just one smell long enough to identify it, can be a very satisfying way to pass some time.

If you push yourself up from your seat in the grass, wait for the blood to flow back into your brain and follow your ear to the edge of the river, you'll find a rocky beach and a deep, gin-clear, teeth-chatteringly cold swimming hole—just right for a mid-summer's day dip. There's an ancient, almost-petrified log next to the pool that invites sitting and the temporary hanging of discarded clothing.

Too infrequently, Annie and I wander down to our secret spot right at dusk when the hawks are returning to their perches in the trees after a full day's hunting, and the owls are starting their night shift prowling for the voles that the hawks left on the table. Dusk is the best time to see wildlife along our undisturbed stretch of the river. The secret spot is alive with activity—the animals here are more tolerant or less aware of our presence for some reason. We stand on the edge of the river and watch the mallards fishing tails-up along the bank while a blue heron beats its long-winged way up river searching out a snack of raw fish before turning in for the night. By the time we head back to the comforts of the farmhouse—a single porch light glowing in the darkness—the stars are flickering high overhead.

Recently we put an old picnic table in the clearing and hacked away enough of the giant thistle to facilitate less painful entry. I also cut away a section of the barbed wire fence to save my privates from the unnerving fear they experienced every time I straddled it to gain access. And just before the hen pheasants settled onto their nests, I mowed a path through the tall grass from the farmhouse down to our secret place. It is now shorts-and-Birkenstocks accessible.

Those are all of the improvements... It has dawned on us that further improvements won't be.

The End

D ear Family, and Friends,
Fellow Walla Wallans,
and Good and Loyal Readers:

I'm sad to say that this is my last letter to you. It has been an interesting ride. I hope you've enjoyed it as much as I have.

This ends the third book about the new lives Annie and I are leading here in Walla Walla. I've just completed what I'm calling my Walla Walla Trilogy. Sounds a little high-blown, doesn't it?

I'm trying out the "trilogy" thing to make my Walla Walla books *sound* important and epic and enduring. (Just so you know, I looked up the definition of the word "trilogy" to make sure that the writing didn't actually have to *be* important, epic or enduring, and thankfully there is no such requirement.)

I'm also hoping that the word "trilogy" will encourage folks to buy all three books as a set, so I can sell more books and get them off of my nap sofa where they are now collecting dust.

And one more thing before I sign off: I feel like I should apologize to you. My books don't do justice to the Walla Walla Valley or the characters who live here. But I want you to know that, however inadequate my efforts, I've done my best to capture some of the wonder of the place.

And hey, how many towns have their own trilogy, anyway?

Thank you for spending a little time with me. I hope to catch up to you again some day.

Best,
SAM

A Brief Update on the McLeod Family

D ear Reader:

You asked for it. Here goes:

Annie is doing quite well as our Farm Boss. She's recently helped deliver two baby alpacas (called "cria"). She's also sold a couple of older animals. So, at this writing, she has 10 alpacas with two more babies on the way. She loves her animals.

The animals are sheared in the spring and Annie has had their fleeces spun into yarn, which is then made into blankets and rugs. These are quite beautiful and very soft.

Summer, our oldest daughter, did get married to her longtime beau, Rusty. The wedding was picture-perfect. It was great to meet Rusty's family and see a lot of old friends. The newlyweds are planning to move to Missoula, Montana in a month or so where Summer will attend graduate school in education and Rusty will work for a couple of years before going on to medical school.

Jolie, our middle child, is in her second year of graduate school in New York City. She, too, is studying to be a teacher and will start her student teaching at an elementary school on the Upper East Side of New York next week.

Marshall, our youngest daughter, is a rising junior in college and is deeply involved in working with primates. She communicates with them through sign language. It is something to see.

I am still writing, doing a good bit of speaking around the Northwest, and working with a former partner to start up another small venture capital fund. I'm afraid it's in my blood.

Best,
SAM

Sam McLeod

Sam McLeod was born in Nashville, Tennessee in 1951, grew up there, attended college and graduate school at The University of Virginia and Washington & Lee University, worked as a banker, a lawyer and a venture capital investor, and retired to Walla Walla, Washington with his wife Annie in 2004. Sam has written three books—*Welcome to Walla Walla, Bottled Walla,* and this book, *Blue Walla.* I'm guessing that he'll keep on writing. We'll see...

For more information on Sam McLeod, his books, Detour Farm, and other important stuff, log on to www.lettersfromwallawalla.com